San Antonio Cooks

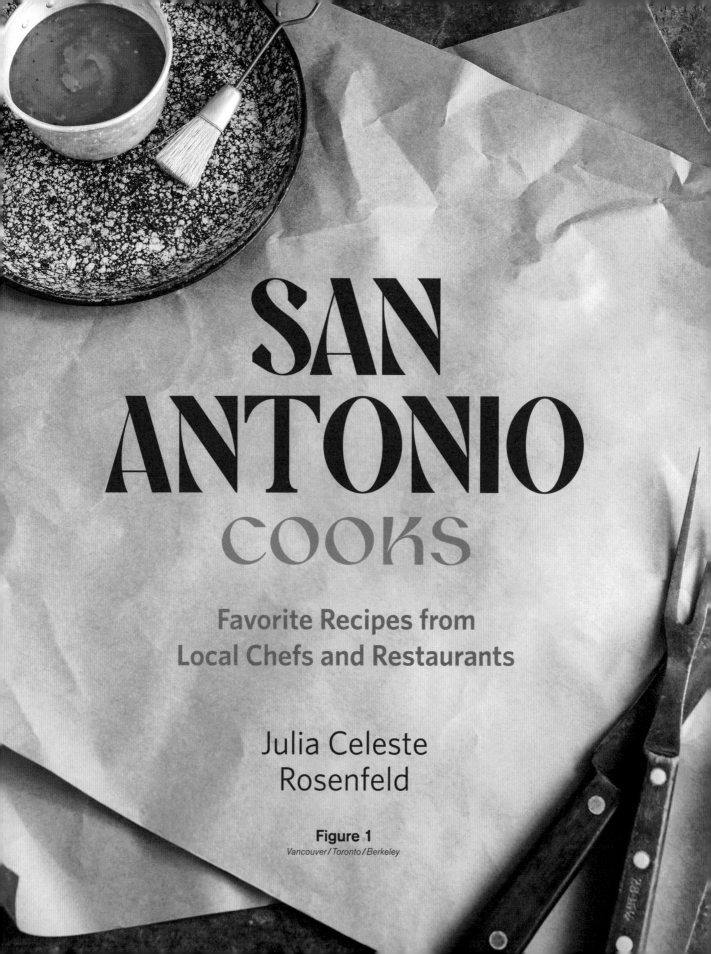

SAN ANTONIO

COOKS

**Favorite Recipes from
Local Chefs and Restaurants**

Julia Celeste
Rosenfeld

Figure 1
Vancouver / Toronto / Berkeley

To my father, Morris, who taught me the difference between eating to live and living to eat. May those of us who know the difference relish every morsel.

22 23 24 25 26   5 4 3 2 1

Cataloguing data is available from Library and Archives Canada
ISBN 978-1-77327-179-8 (hbk.)

Design by Teresa Bubela
Photography by Jessica Attie
Food and prop styling by Ali Mendez Clayton

Editing by Michelle Meade
Copy editing by Marnie Lamb
Proofreading by Breanne MacDonald
Indexing by Iva Cheung

Printed and bound in China by C&C Offset Printing Co.
Distributed internationally by Publishers Group West

Figure 1 Publishing Inc.
Vancouver BC Canada
www.figure1publishing.com

Figure 1 Publishing works in the traditional, unceded territory of the Xʷməθkʷəy̓əm (Musqueam), Skwxwú7mesh (Squamish) and Səl̓ílwətaʔɬ (Tsleil-Waututh) peoples.

RECIPE NOTES

Unless stated otherwise:

Butter is unsalted.

Herbs are fresh.

Eggs are large.

Sugar is granulated.

Black pepper is freshly ground.

Contents

Introduction

This book is about resilience. About creativity and courage in the face of abrupt change. About unerring drive for one's passion, devotion to people, and heritage. It is about gastronomic awareness, ingredient integrity, and unwavering hospitality. It is a love letter to San Antonio's food and the dedicated artists who decorate our restaurant tables with their flavor palates and color palettes in full view.

The COVID-19 outbreak was a game-changing, life-altering, business-stressing global event. Everyone felt the strain, and restaurants and bars felt it deeply. Those in this book are the survivors and optimists who see a clear path forward. Some have been in business for decades, others are in their sophomore years, and a handful of them opened during the pandemic. All are fighters who want to present their very best food to anyone who wants it. It's that simple.

San Antonio suffers from a Hollywood-driven image of the city's olden days: a sleepy, dusty town with the Alamo center stage, open-air taco stands on every corner, and colorful cantinas serving shots of whiskey to men and salt-rimmed glasses of margaritas to women. The soundtrack is mariachi music, and just past the Riverwalk, tumbleweed rolls through the streets.

Record scratch.

This is an expanding, modern city, the seventh largest in the United States. Thanks to our warm weather, charming historical architecture, friendly locals, and general affordability, we delight in being a tourist town. Our rich and thriving dining scene has everything from a family-run taqueria serving quick breakfast tacos to a formidable fine-dining restaurant offering a chef-led experience. San Antonio is the top destination for in-state vacations, and travel magazines frequently rank it as one of the best U.S. cities to visit. Visit once, and you'll visit again.

Those of us in and around the restaurant industry know our food keeps people coming back for more. You could say the Chili Queens in San Antonio's busy 1860s plazas were the first to beckon visitors to our city's tables, enticing them with the aromatic stew of exotic spices, precious meat, and local produce, dishing up what we now know as chili con carne. Their spirits remain in our Tex-Mex staples; the allure of the flavors takes root in the soul.

As a UNESCO City of Gastronomy, San Antonio honors those women pioneers, as well as the indigenous groups, the conquering Spanish and adventurous Canary Islanders, the freed slaves, and the freedom-seeking European immigrants who have infused their cultures into our customs and flavors.

More than three hundred years of history and heritage have shaped our cuisine. A wonderfully original food region has grown and evolved because of, and through, these communities. New breeds of seeds, including cumin, traveled here in the pockets of Canary Islanders, while indigenous groups shared their success in cultivating the three sisters of corn, squash, and beans. The Spanish introduced their ancient irrigation techniques that extended the growing seasons. They also brought horses and cattle to the endless acres of open land, creating ranching practices that continue today. Germans and Poles brought their meat-smoking and sausage-making skills, now an iconic element of Texas cuisine. Working together, the early settlers adapted their new world from what they knew and what they learned.

In 1979, one of my first freelance jobs after college graduation was writing about San Antonio's restaurants. The editor wanted a business slant on dining, so I wrote about openings, relocations, success stories, and the latest dinner-theater shows. The pay was dreadful, but it put me on a focused path of researching and understanding the makings of memorable meals, elevated fine-dining experiences, and restaurant successes. I attended cooking classes to learn about ingredients and techniques, and I worked as a server to understand hospitality and service from the inside.

Much later, my fourteen years as the restaurant reviewer for *San Antonio Magazine* provided me with unique insights into the industry's personalities and quirks. As the local *Zagat* editor, I quickly translated the language used by customers to express their

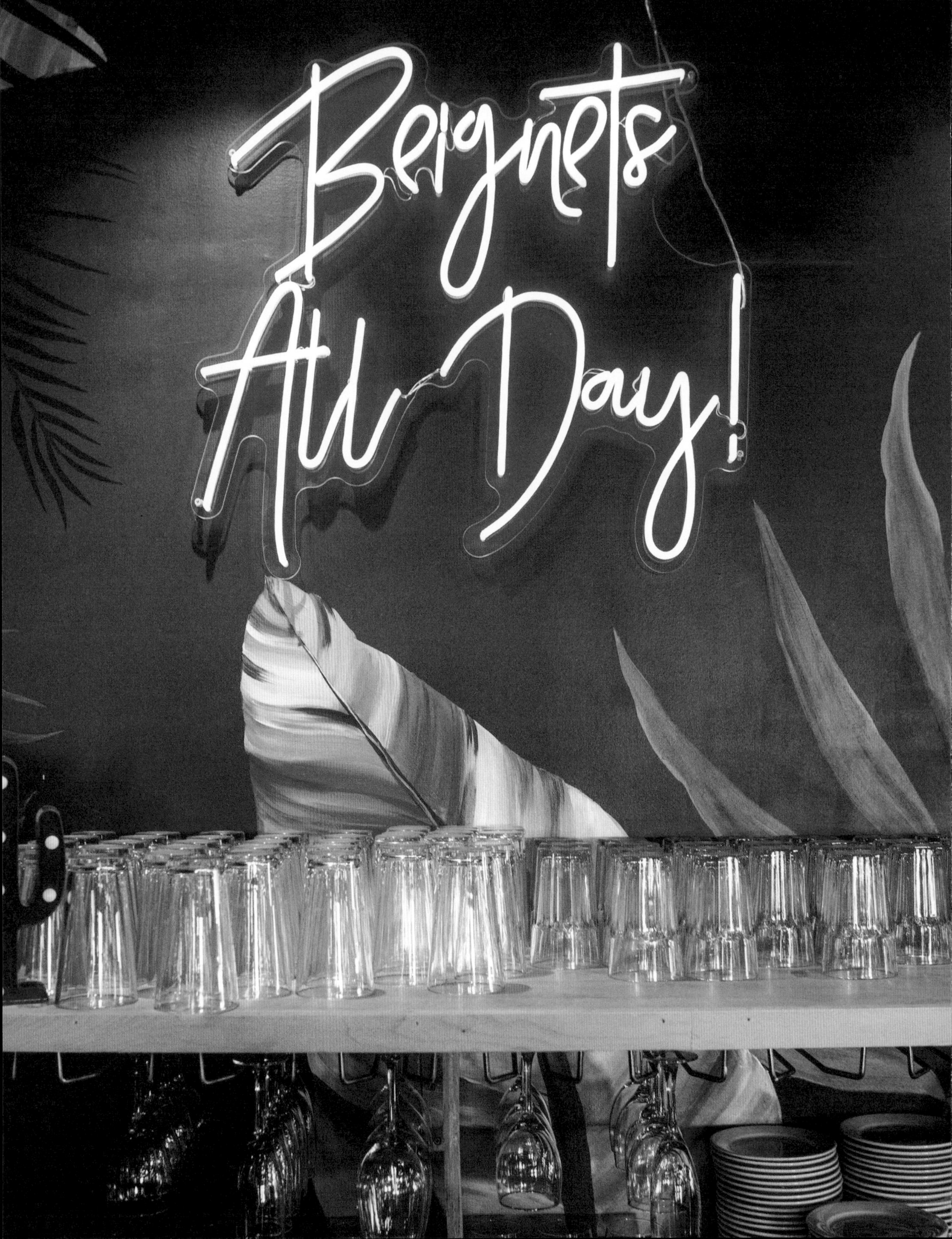
Beignets
All Day!

best (and worst) restaurant experiences. Today, my Food Chick Tours business offers me yet another opportunity: to redefine tourism through our food and history. Along the way, I've had the pleasure of being invited into the kitchens and the lives of the chefs I've grown to know well and admire greatly.

What I respect most about our chefs is their passion for an exhausting and often financially draining business, filled with never-ending repetition of menial yet essential tasks and an endless quest for perfection in every step. They take feedback personally: even a series of standing ovations can be overshadowed by a single boo. Closing for the pandemic made some stronger and others fall to their knees. Yet up they get. And on they go.

While some of our Spanish Colonial missions and UNESCO World Heritage sites remain our physical link to then, make no mistake, this book is about *now*.

San Antonio's dining scene has risen beyond spicy stews and corn tortillas. Here, you'll find Moroccan, French, Chinese, Japanese, Caribbean, Korean, New Orleanian, and classic Continental cuisines. Even within those labels, you'll find creative inventions from the minds of chefs who love to eat. And isn't that the goal of life? To enjoy what we do and share that pleasure with others? Let's dig in.

The Restaurants

The Recipes

2M Smokehouse

Esaul Ramos (R)
and Joe Melig (L)

THE MYSTIQUE of Texas barbecue has made legends of many. Among them is pitmaster Esaul Ramos, who co-owns and operates 2M Smokehouse with his high school buddy Joe Melig. A broadly painted exterior sign boasts "BBQ con ganas," a colloquialism broadly meaning "BBQ with vigor." Since opening 2M Smokehouse in 2016, the pair have demonstrated their vitality, equaled only by the zeal of the fans who line up to order. After all, this barbecue is as close as you can get to the masterful expression of backyard smoking and heritage kitchen cookery, both passed through generations of skillful Mexican American hands. The screened smokehouse, prep tables, dining tables, and patios were handmade by Melig, Ramos, and their families and friends. And that laser focus on craft carries into every morsel of meat, every link of house-made sausage, and every side.

Mexi-Q, as some locals call it, is the Mexican interpretation of this cowboy cuisine. Here, the sides have the accents: the mac 'n' cheese is topped with a layer of crisp chicharrones, the beans are south-of-the-border ranchero-style, and one of the salad options is pickled nopales (cactus paddles). You can even ask for spicy pico de gallo instead of BBQ sauce.

While the smoked meats don't roam far from the Texas classic of salt and pepper rubs and slow-smoking tradition, the barbacoa offered on the first Sunday of every month adds another passionate example of how Ramos and Melig honor family and heritage.

Smoked Turkey Breast SERVES 4–6

While all the barbecue meats are popular at this busy restaurant, this succulent smoked turkey breast is known for its deep, smoky, and honeyed flavor and is a notable highlight.

3 Tbsp kosher salt

7 Tbsp black pepper

4–6 lbs boneless, skinless turkey breast

2 cups warm honey (divided)

2 cups (4 sticks) butter, melted and kept warm

Set the smoker temperature to 240°F–250°F.

Mix salt and pepper in a small bowl. Evenly season meat with a thin layer of the mixture. (If there's a thin point of meat on one end of the breast, tuck it under the larger area.) Place turkey on the grates of the smoker, close the lid, and smoke for 2 hours, until golden on top.

Transfer meat to a tray and pour 1 cup honey on top. Return turkey to the smoker, without the tray, and close the lid. Smoke for another 1 hour, or until turkey reaches an internal temperature of 100°F–110°F.

Place turkey on a large sheet of aluminum foil and pour remaining 1 cup honey on top. Wrap tightly and return to the smoker. Increase the temperature to 280°F and smoke for another hour, until turkey reaches an internal temperature of 145°F at its center. Remove turkey from the smoker and set aside to rest for 20 minutes in the foil.

Slice the rested turkey and brush with warm butter. If serving sliced turkey over an extended period of time, keep the slices in a lidded container with warm butter, brushing often to retain turkey's moisture.

Mexican Street Corn SERVES 4–6

The Mexican chili-lime seasoning Tajin is an essential *elote* (street corn) topping, but it's also delicious sprinkled over fruit, veggies, and meats. It can generally be found in the produce department of grocery stores or in the Mexican specialty foods aisle.

Preheat a grill or smoker over high heat. (Alternatively, preheat a cast-iron skillet on a stovetop.)

Lightly rub oil over corn. Place corn on the heated grill (or skillet) and roast for 10 minutes, turning frequently to prevent burning. Set aside to cool.

Shave kernels off the cob and measure out 4 cups. Set aside.

Melt butter in a large saucepan over medium heat. Stir in milk and easy-melt cheese until smooth. Mix in corn kernels, then season with salt and pepper. Stir in crema (or sour cream) until warmed through.

Pour into a serving bowl, then top with cotija cheese and sprinklings of Tajin.

¼ cup corn oil
8 ears fresh corn, husk and silk removed
2 cups (4 sticks) butter
1 cup whole milk
2 cups easy-melt cheese (preferably Velveeta)
Kosher salt and black pepper, to taste
½ cup Mexican crema or sour cream
¼–½ cup grated cotija cheese
Tajin, for sprinkling

Bakery Lorraine

Anne Ng (c),
Jeremy Mandrell (R),
and Blake Hutcherson (L)

FOR BAKERS, co-owners, and life partners Anne Ng and Jeremy Mandrell, it's been a winding road to what is now their San Antonio baking empire. They first met on the overnight shift at Bouchon Bakery in Yountville, California, in the kitchen of esteemed chef Thomas Keller. Both left baking for brief stints in the tech industry but eventually returned to the baking world, where their hearts belonged. They worked multiple jobs as they established their new bakery (including weekend mornings at a farmer's market), slept on a cot in the bakery's kitchen to tend to overnight bakes, and sought out enough reliable staff to help the business grow.

Their creatively flavored and meticulously perfected French macarons—grapefruit/ginger, horchata, mojito, cereal milk, and Arnold Palmer, to name a few—as well as their flaky and buttery croissants were met with rave reviews. Fast-forward ten years later: the business now includes four Bakery Lorraine bakery-cafés across San Antonio, one in Austin, and a central baking facility to support the volume of business. The quality pastries, breads, and patisserie items still draw in crowds, and with executive chef Blake Hutcherson overseeing the café menu, Bakery Lorraine has become a go-to for full sit-down breakfasts and lunches too.

The success couldn't come to nicer people. Ng and Mandrell are committed to their community, giving back through charitable donations and working as volunteer cooks in disaster zones for Mercy Chefs. Great things do happen to talented, hardworking people.

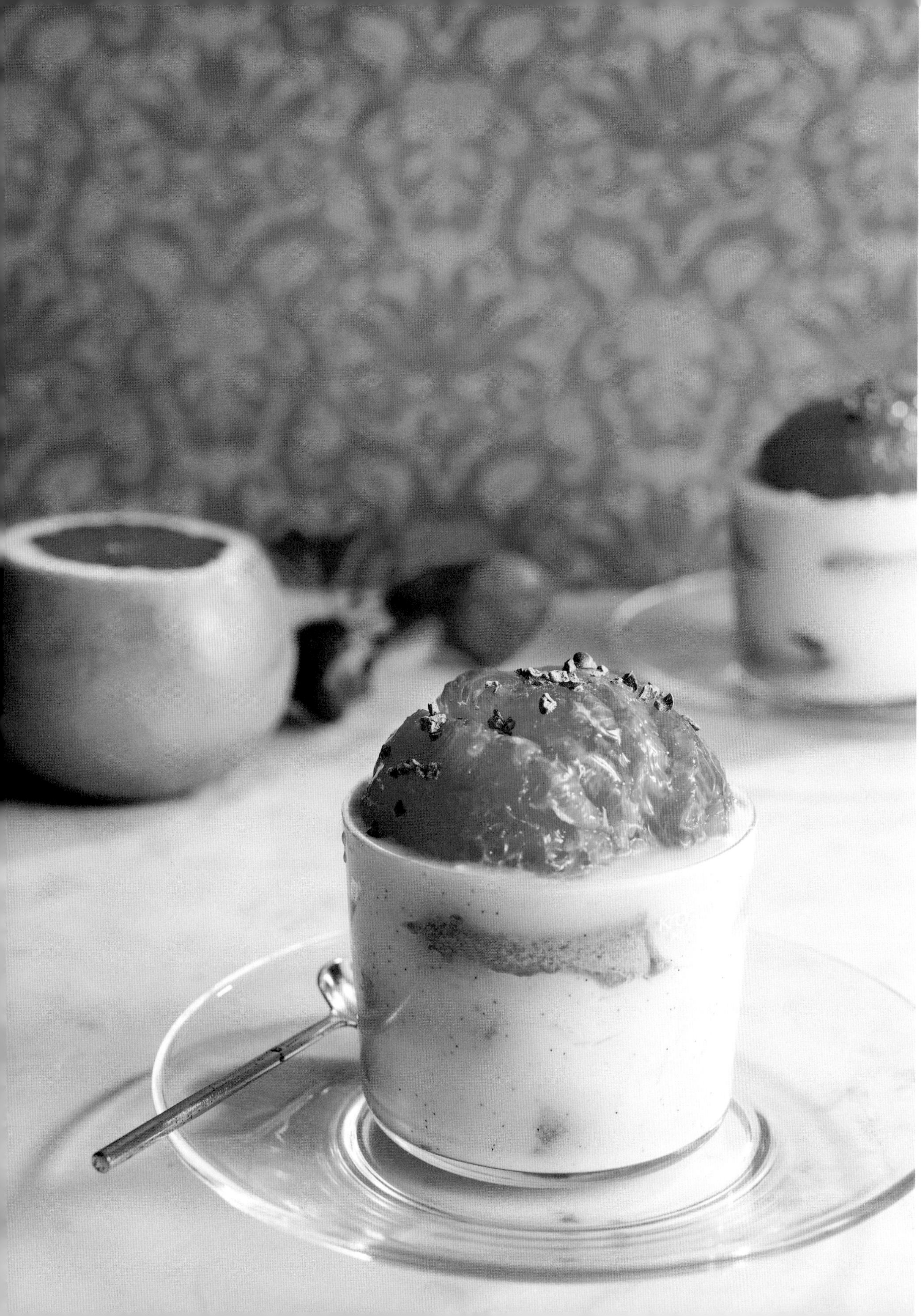

BAKERY LORRAINE Grapefruit Tiramisu, p. 24

Grits with Tomato Gravy and Fried Egg SERVES 4–6

Executive chef Blake Hutcherson says, "Grits are ground from dried dent corn, a variety of corn that is starchier and less sweet than summertime corn on the cob. We use freshly ground grits from Texas-grown heritage dent corn (sourced from Barton Springs Mill) so that the flavor and aroma of corn remains at the forefront of this dish."

GRITS

2 cups grits
2 bay leaves
3 Tbsp butter
1 Tbsp Crystal hot sauce
1 Tbsp kosher salt (preferably Morton's)
2 tsp black pepper
½ cup shredded Gruyère cheese

TOMATO BROTH

1 Tbsp olive oil
1 shallot, coarsely chopped
1 Tbsp tomato paste
3 cups canned crushed tomatoes with juice
3 bay leaves
1 tsp kosher salt
1 tsp black pepper

GRITS Bring 2 quarts water to a boil in a stockpot over high heat. Using a whisk, stir in grits. Reduce to low heat and simmer. Add bay leaves and stir often to prevent grits from burning or sticking to the bottom of the pot. Cook grits for 30 minutes, until tender and soft. Stir in butter, hot sauce, salt, and pepper and taste. Adjust seasoning if needed.

Remove from heat, discard bay leaves, and stir in cheese until well mixed. Keep warm.

TOMATO BROTH Heat oil in a medium saucepan over medium heat. Add shallots and sauté for 2 minutes, until fragrant. Add tomato paste and stir until it begins to darken and caramelize. Be careful not to burn the mixture as it cooks. Reduce heat if necessary.

Add 3 cups water and stir to deglaze pan. Add tomatoes and bay leaves and stir. Bring to a boil, then reduce to low heat and simmer for 30 minutes, until the liquid has reduced by a third. Stir in salt and pepper.

Strain the mixture through a fine-mesh sieve into another saucepan, pressing the back of a ladle into the mixture to extract more flavor. Discard solids and keep broth warm. If not using immediately, cool completely and store in a covered container in the refrigerator.

TOMATO GRAVY Heat a cast-iron skillet over high heat. Place lemon, cut side down, into the skillet and sear for up to 5 minutes, until charred. Remove and set aside.

Heat a deep skillet over high heat. Add bacon and cook for 4–6 minutes, until fat is rendered and bacon begins to brown. Add okra and sauté for another 4–5 minutes, until okra is browned. Stir in shallots and cook for 2 minutes, until fragrant. Add garlic and sauté for another minute, until fragrant.

Averting your face to avoid the splatter, carefully pour in tomato broth and add lemon. Reduce to low heat and simmer for 8 minutes, until sauce has reduced by a third. Remove lemon and discard. Season with salt and pepper. Keep gravy warm.

FRIED EGG Heat oil in a nonstick skillet over medium heat. Crack an egg into the pan, being careful not to break yolk, and cook for 2 minutes, until egg white is set and browned on the sides. Season with salt and pepper. If needed, spoon some oil over egg white as it cooks to prevent yolk from overcooking.

Transfer to a plate. Repeat with remaining eggs. Keep warm.

ASSEMBLY Ladle ¾ cup grits into each serving bowl. Spoon ¼–½ cup tomato gravy on top, making sure to include bacon and okra in each bowl. Top with a fried egg and garnish with scallions.

TOMATO GRAVY

½ lemon

3–4 large slices bacon, diced into ½-inch pieces (¼ cup)

1 cup okra, cut into ½-inch slices

1 large shallot, finely chopped (½ cup)

3 cloves garlic, minced

2 cups Tomato Broth (see here)

1 Tbsp kosher salt (preferably Morton's)

2 tsp black pepper

FRIED EGG

1 tsp neutral oil such as canola, plus extra if needed

4–6 eggs

Kosher salt and black pepper

ASSEMBLY

Grits (see here)

Tomato Gravy (see here)

Fried Egg (see here)

1 scallion, finely chopped, for garnish

Grapefruit Tiramisu   SERVES 12

Grapefruit trees grow throughout San Antonio's older neighborhoods, and orchards of them produce a big cash crop export for the Rio Grande Valley a few hours south of the city. If you can find them, Ruby Red grapefruits add a beautiful pop of color to this dessert. And to save time, you can use store-bought ladyfingers.

LADYFINGERS

4 eggs, separated (200 g)
⅔ cup sugar (130 g) (divided)
⅓ tsp cream of tartar (1 g)
½ tsp egg white powder (1 g)
   (available in baking aisles)
⅔ cup all-purpose flour (80 g)

CRÈME ANGLAISE

2 tsp powdered gelatin (4–5 g)
2 vanilla beans, halved lengthwise
1¼ cups + 2½ Tbsp heavy cream
   (333 g)
6½ Tbsp sugar (85 g)
4–5 egg yolks (65 g)

LADYFINGERS Preheat convection oven to 375°F. Line a baking sheet with parchment paper.

In a large bowl, combine egg yolks and ⅓ cup (70 g) sugar and whip for 5 minutes, until fluffy and almost white.

In a separate bowl, combine egg whites, cream of tartar, egg white powder, and 3 tablespoons (40 g) sugar and whisk until stiff peaks form. Sift flour onto the whipped yolk mixture, then gently fold in. Lightly fold in the egg white mixture.

Spoon mixture into a piping bag fitted with a large plain tip. Pipe out 5- x 1½-inch batons of batter onto the baking sheet, evenly spacing them ½-inch apart. Sprinkle remaining 1½ tablespoons (20 g) sugar over top.

Bake for 12 minutes, or until light brown and crusty. Remove from oven and set the baking sheet aside to cool completely. If not using ladyfingers immediately, store in an airtight container. When ready to use, place ladyfingers on a baking sheet in a 225°F oven for 1 hour to dry out before building the tiramisu.

CRÈME ANGLAISE Pour 2 tablespoons water into a small bowl and sprinkle gelatin on top, stirring to distribute gelatin evenly. Set aside to bloom for 3–5 minutes.

Scrape the seeds of the vanilla beans into a saucepan. Add the empty pods and cream. Bring to a boil over medium-high heat, then reduce to low heat and gently simmer.

Fill a large bowl with ice water.

Meanwhile, combine sugar and egg yolks in a bowl and whisk. Pour in half of the hot cream, a little at a time, and whisk continuously. Pour all of the egg yolk mixture into the saucepan of hot cream and keep warm on low heat. Using a wooden spoon, slowly and continuously stir the mixture until it reaches 185°F. The mixture should be thick enough to coat the back of the spoon.

Turn off the heat, add the bloomed gelatin mixture, and stir until completely dissolved. Strain the mixture through a fine-mesh sieve into a large metal bowl. Place the bowl in the ice water bath and cool.

MASCARPONE CREAM Place mascarpone in a large bowl. Using a whisk, gently and slowly add in crème anglaise, a little at a time, until smooth. (Take care: if you whisk too aggressively, you might curdle the cheese.) Fold in the whipped cream.

GRAPEFRUIT SYRUP Combine all ingredients in a saucepan and heat over medium heat, stirring until sugar has dissolved. Cool to room temperature.

GRAPEFRUIT SUPREMES Trim off the top and bottom of a grapefruit. Set cut side up on a cutting board. Carefully slice lengthwise between flesh and peel, following fruit's contour to remove the peel and pith.

Hold the fruit over a bowl to catch the juice or place on a cutting board. Cut out each segment, between the membranes. (The segments are called *supremes*.) Repeat with remaining grapefruits.

ASSEMBLY Set out a 3-quart rectangular serving dish or 12 (8-ounce) individual dishes. Spread a light layer of mascarpone cream on the bottom, just enough to cover the dish. Dip a ladyfinger into the grapefruit syrup for a few seconds, then immediately place over the cream. (If making individual portions, cut the ladyfingers into smaller pieces before dipping in syrup.) Repeat the process until the cream is covered in a single layer of ladyfingers.

Spread half of remaining cream over ladyfingers, then repeat the layering process. Finish with a layer of cream, then refrigerate for at least 1 hour to set.

In a small bowl, toss cocoa nibs in gold dust (if using). Arrange the supremes on top of the cream layer. Garnish with gold-dusted cocoa nibs, then serve.

MASCARPONE CREAM

375 g mascarpone cheese
(about 1⅔ cups)
Crème Anglaise, cooled (see here)
¾ cup + 2 Tbsp heavy cream,
whipped to soft peaks (215 g)

GRAPEFRUIT SYRUP

2 cups freshly squeezed grapefruit
juice (500 g)
1 cup + 2 Tbsp sugar (225 g)
Zest of 2 grapefruits

GRAPEFRUIT SUPREMES

4 large grapefruits

ASSEMBLY

Mascarpone Cream (see here)
Ladyfingers (see here)
Grapefruit Syrup (see here)
¼ cup cocoa nibs (optional)
1 Tbsp edible gold luster dust
(optional)
Grapefruit Supremes (see here)

Battalion

Josh Davis

THIS 1924 two-story firehouse sat empty for years on a prime corner in hip Southtown/King William, but it hasn't seen a neglected day since Battalion owner Andrew Goodman completed the loving renovation in 2017. Some of the coolest original elements of the fire station remain, including the poles, tall arched windows, and huge garage doors, but the décor is certainly not drab. It's glittery glam kitsch with pops of fire-truck red, acrylic, and mood lighting.

And the menu is on fire under the watch of executive chef Josh Davis, who puts his spin on traditional Italian dishes. A light veggie lasagna is prepared with layers of locally sourced savoy cabbage, beets, and chèvre, while a fresh butterleaf salad is upgraded with fried pepperoni and crispy garlic crunch. Davis may weave in a hyper-local approach to the straightforward menu, but he remains true to the foundations of Italian cuisine by including plenty of traditional handmade pastas and beautifully grilled meats. The theme of the bar is decidedly firefighter chic with punchy flavors from cocktails such as the absinthe-touched Jaws of Life and the spirited Campari-Tequila Arsonist.

While you won't be allowed to slide down the fire pole, you can take a ride in the glass elevator—which is just another element of whimsy in this dinnertime firehouse experience.

Grilled Street Corn Cavatelli SERVES 4

This dish was inspired by chef Davis's love of street corn and its prominence in San Antonio. If you're not up to making the pasta, use prepared orecchiette or shells to capture sauce in every bite.

PAPRIKA-LIME CAVATELLI In a stand mixer fitted with the hook attachment, combine ricotta, eggs, lime zest, paprika, kosher salt, and flour and mix on medium-low speed until a soft and slightly sticky dough is formed. (Alternatively, mix by hand in a large bowl.) If needed, add more flour to get the right texture.

Remove the dough to a work surface and form into a ball. Dust with flour and wrap in plastic wrap. Set aside to rest for 30 minutes at room temperature.

Line a baking sheet with parchment paper.

Dust a clean cutting board or work surface with flour. Flour the dough. Using a rolling pin, roll the dough into a round or rectangle, about ½-inch thick. Cut ½-inch-wide strips from the dough, dust each lightly with flour, and roll them gently into cylinders. Cut out 1-inch pieces. Roll each piece on a gnocchi board (see page 78). (Alternatively, use fork tines to make grooves on one side. Then, use your fingertips to form a hollow curved piece of pasta.) Place finished pasta on the baking sheet.

In a stockpot, combine a gallon of water and ¼ cup salt and bring to a boil. Working in batches to avoid overcrowding, gently lower cavatelli into the pot and cook for 2 minutes, until soft but not doughy. Using a slotted spoon, transfer pasta into a large bowl. Add a drizzle of oil and toss. Reserve 1½ cups pasta water for the sauce. Any uncooked cavatelli can be stored in the refrigerator for up to 5 days or in the freezer for a month.

GRILLED STREET CORN SAUCE Preheat a cast-iron grill or frying pan over medium-high heat. Lightly rub corn with oil and grill for 10–12 minutes, until slightly charred. Set aside until cool to the touch.

Shave kernels into a bowl.

Heat a skillet over medium heat. Add corn, chipotle, and pasta water and bring to a simmer.

ASSEMBLY Add cavatelli to sauce. Mix in butter until fully incorporated. Season with lime juice and salt, then adjust seasoning to taste. Stir once more and plate. Garnish generously with cotija (or Parmesan) and cilantro.

Serve immediately.

PAPRIKA-LIME CAVATELLI

2 cups whole-milk ricotta
2 eggs
Zest of 2 limes
2 tsp smoked paprika
Kosher salt
4 cups all-purpose flour, plus extra if needed and for dusting
¼ cup salt
Olive oil, for drizzling

GRILLED STREET CORN SAUCE

2 ears corn, shucked
Corn oil
2–4 Tbsp chipotle peppers in adobo sauce, puréed
1½ cups reserved pasta water

ASSEMBLY

Paprika-Lime Cavatelli (see here)
Grilled Street Corn Sauce (see here)
¼ cup (½ stick) butter, cubed
Juice of 1 lime
Kosher salt
Grated cotija cheese or Parmesan, for garnish
½ bunch cilantro, chopped, for garnish

Square Meatballs with Quick Tomato Sauce SERVES 6–8

This signature appetizer at Battalion has been on the menu since opening day. It's also a great party dish that can be prepared in advance.

MEATBALLS Line a 9- x 13-inch casserole dish with parchment paper.

In a large bowl, combine all ingredients and mix with your hands. Place the meat mixture in the dish and press into an even layer. Refrigerate for 2 hours.

QUICK TOMATO SAUCE Heat oil in a large saucepan over medium-low heat. Add garlic and sauté for 2 minutes, until golden brown. Add oregano and gently sauté for 10 seconds. Averting your face, carefully add tomatoes (they will splatter), then season lightly with salt and pepper. Simmer over low heat for 30 minutes, stirring occasionally, until sauce has thickened. Add vinegar and sugar, then season to taste with salt and pepper. Any leftover sauce can be stored in an airtight container in the freezer for up to 6 months and enjoyed with any pasta.

ASSEMBLY Heat oil in a skillet over medium heat. Cut meat mixture into 1½-inch squares. Working in batches to avoid overcrowding, add the squares to the pan. Sear for 5 minutes on each side, until a crust forms. Drain meatballs on a rack.

Place a ladle of sauce into each serving plate or shallow bowl. Add 2–3 meatballs to each, then top with Parmesan and basil.

MEATBALLS
1 lb ground beef
1 lb ground pork
3 cloves garlic, minced
¼ white onion, minced
½ bunch Italian parsley, leaves only and finely chopped
Sprig of oregano, leaves only and finely chopped
1½ cups grated mozzarella
¾ cup finely grated Parmesan
½ cup breadcrumbs
2½ tsp kosher salt
2½ tsp black pepper
1 egg, beaten
Zest and juice of 1 lemon

QUICK TOMATO SAUCE
¼ cup olive oil
10 cloves garlic, thinly sliced
3 sprigs oregano, leaves only and finely chopped
2 (28-oz) cans diced or crushed tomatoes
Kosher salt and black pepper, to taste
2 Tbsp red wine vinegar
1 Tbsp sugar

ASSEMBLY
1–2 Tbsp canola oil
Meatballs (see here)
Quick Tomato Sauce (see here)
Finely grated Parmesan
¼ cup chopped or whole leaves basil

Best Quality Daughter

Jennifer Hwa Dobbertin and Quealy Watson

THE NAME refers to a tender moment between a Chinese mother and her first-generation American-born daughter in Amy Tan's novel *The Joy Luck Club*; the restaurant is an ode to the similarly complicated relationship that chef-owner Jennifer Hwa Dobbertin has with her Chinese-born mother. After years of traveling and living in Asia, Dobbertin and co-owner/chef Quealy Watson created this culinary love note to China, Southeast Asia, and South Texas, all wokked together in an exciting medley of choices, spices, and fun.

The exhilarating décor will first grab your gaze. The chinoiserie wallpaper is bright pink in one dining room, vibrant blue in another, and customized with San Antonio landmarks sprinkled into the jade green design in the bar. The menu—part travel guide and part memories of Dobbertin's childhood comfort foods—pulls together an artful blend of umami and zest that reflects tradition and innovation in every dish. It requires the minds of two chefs, their skilled palates, and imagination to develop these unique, new Asian American dishes. *Char siu* (BBQ pork) and boudin-seasoned rice are tucked into egg rolls. Shaved ribbons of summer squash are tossed with miso ricotta and chrysanthemum vinegar. Colorful cocktails layer butterfly pea flower syrup, lychee, lemongrass, and house-made shrubs. It adds up to serious food and drink that doesn't take itself seriously but would make any mother proud.

Char Siu Pork in Bao Buns with Sesame Hoisin and Pickled Red Onions SERVES 4–6

PICKLED RED ONIONS

2 red onions, thinly sliced
2 cups white vinegar
½ cup Shaoxing rice wine
½ cup sugar
¼ tsp kosher salt
1 bay leaf

CHAR SIU MARINADE

8 cloves garlic, minced
1 (2-inch) piece ginger, finely chopped
½ cup brown sugar
2 Tbsp beet powder or dash of red food coloring (optional)
1 tsp five-spice powder
½ tsp white pepper
1½ cups oyster sauce
1 cup soy sauce
1 cup Shaoxing rice wine
½ cup honey
4 lbs boneless pork shoulder, cut into 2-inch strips or chunks

CHAR SIU PORK GLAZE

2 cups honey
¼ cup Char Siu Marinade (see here)
1 tsp beet powder or dash of red food coloring (optional)

SESAME HOISIN SAUCE

½ cup oyster sauce
½ cup hoisin sauce
¼ cup sesame oil

ASSEMBLY

12 bao buns (available in most Asian grocery stores) or small tortillas
Char Siu Pork (see here)
Pickled Red Onions (see here)
Sesame Hoisin Sauce (see here)
Bunch of cilantro and/or Thai basil, leaves only
Bunch of scallions, thinly sliced diagonally

PICKLED RED ONIONS Pack onions into a 1-quart mason jar or any lidded container large enough to hold them.

Place remaining ingredients and ½ cup water in a medium saucepan and bring to a simmer over medium heat. Stir until sugar has dissolved. Pour pickling liquid over onions and set aside to cool. Refrigerate until needed. Pickled red onions can be stored in the refrigerator for up to a month.

CHAR SIU MARINADE In a large bowl, combine all ingredients except pork and mix well. Reserve ¼ cup for later use. Add pork to the bowl and mix well. Cover and refrigerate for at least 4 hours and up to 24 hours.

CHAR SIU PORK GLAZE In a bowl, whisk all ingredients together. Set aside.

CHAR SIU PORK Preheat oven to 475°F.

Place a baking rack in a roasting pan. Pour water into the pan to just below the surface of the rack. Lay marinated pork across the rack. (The water prevents the drippings from burning.)

Roast for 10 minutes. Reduce oven temperature to 400°F and roast for another 20 minutes. Flip pork pieces, then rotate the pan 180 degrees to ensure even cooking. Roast for 10 minutes. (If the pork edges are burning, reduce the temperature to 350°F–375°F.)

Remove the pan from the oven and baste both sides of pork with glaze. Roast for 10 minutes, then baste again. Roast for a final 5–10 minutes, until char siu is sticky, caramelized, and if it's your thing, slightly charred on the tips. Set aside to rest.

SESAME HOISIN SAUCE In a bowl, whisk all ingredients and ¼ cup water until well combined. Set aside and stir before serving.

ASSEMBLY Warm bao buns (or tortillas) in a steamer or oven. Place on a plate.

Slice pork into ¼-inch-thick slices and transfer to a serving plate. Serve pork with bao buns, drained pickled red onions, sesame hoisin sauce, cilantro (and/or Thai basil), and scallions.

Thai Crab Curry Fried Rice SERVES 4

Crab curry is a popular Thai dish, unique in that it uses curry powder instead of the usual curry paste found in other Thai curries. The fried rice version of this dish is traditionally served at beaches alongside a bucket of ice-cold beer.

FRIED RICE SAUCE Combine all ingredients and ¼ cup water in a food processor. Pulse until combined. Set aside.

FRIED RICE Heat oil in a large wok or skillet over medium heat. Add garlic and ginger and sauté for 1 minute, until fragrant. Add eggs and lightly scramble. Increase to high heat and stir in rice, crab, scallions, and enough sauce to just coat the rice. (Overcrowding the pan can steam the rice and cause it to be mushy. If necessary, work in batches.)

   Using a wooden spoon, break up the chunks of rice and egg until everything is evenly incorporated. Take care not to break up the crab. Stir-fry for 2 minutes.

   Transfer to a serving plate, add a squeeze of lime, and garnish with cilantro.

FRIED RICE SAUCE
2 cloves garlic, peeled
1½ Tbsp curry powder
1 Tbsp chopped ginger
1 Tbsp crab paste with soybean oil
   (found in Asian supermarkets)
3 Tbsp fish sauce
1 Tbsp Golden Mountain Seasoning
   Sauce or soy sauce

FRIED RICE
3 Tbsp canola oil
6 cloves garlic, minced
1 Tbsp finely chopped ginger
2 eggs, beaten
3 cups day-old cooked rice, left in
   fridge overnight on a pan to dry out
6 oz best-quality crabmeat or
   lump crab (see Note)
3 scallions, roughly chopped
Fried Rice Sauce (see here)
Lime wedges
Cilantro, for garnish

NOTE >> We recommend high-quality crab since it's the star of the show.

Biga on the Banks

Bruce Auden

THEMATIC TASTING menus, prix-fixe specials, Riverwalk dining—these are the elements that make locals loyal and visitors thrilled about Biga on the Banks. Chef Bruce Auden is widely recognized as one of the pioneering chefs of Southwestern cuisine and always placed at the top of the city's list of best chefs (plus, he's been a James Beard Award nominee for Best Chef Southwest ten years in a row).

"Old Biga," as regulars still call it, broke culinary ground in 1991 with nouvelle American and regional cuisine. Auden's dishes included sizzling platters of wild and cultivated mushrooms, quail, antelope, and signature sticky toffee pudding with English custard, while crusty loaves of artisan bread on every table were baked in the adjacent LocuStreet Bakery. In 2000, they moved to the grander Biga on the Banks, set above a quiet stretch of Riverwalk, expanding the opportunity to indulge to a wider audience. Here, billowing fabric and artistically placed gourds separate banquettes and intimate dining areas, the narrow outdoor patio overlooks the river below, and the level of culinary excellence continues to rise well above the norm, with dishes such as habanero jerk scallops, 11-spiced venison, and chef's signature chicken-fried oysters. Biga's luxurious yet casual bent is inclusive: it's a come-as-you-like dining room where visitors in jeans are as welcome as glitterati in cocktail attire. And everyone is in for a treat.

Phyllo-Wrapped Snapper with Mustard Leeks, Tomato Jam, and Pinot Sauce SERVES 4 (MAIN COURSE) OR 8 (APPETIZER)

TOMATO JAM In a medium saucepan, combine vinegar, sugar, cinnamon, cloves, and cumin and cook over medium heat for 1 minute. Add tomatoes and cook for 30 minutes. Stir in honey.

Transfer the mixture to a blender and purée for just a few seconds until smooth. Season with salt and pepper.

PHYLLO-WRAPPED SNAPPER Preheat oven to 350°F.

Carefully cut 2 parallel pockets (one over the other) in the side of each fillet. Tuck a slice of ham (or prosciutto) in each pocket. Wrap each fillet in wilted spinach leaves.

On a work surface lightly dusted with flour, lay out a sheet of phyllo dough and brush with melted butter. Cut sheets to the width of the fillets (or leave full size). Roll each fillet in phyllo. If using full sheets, fold over excess dough to make a neat packet. Repeat with 2 more layers of butter-brushed phyllo.

Place packets on a baking sheet and bake for 25 minutes, until golden brown.

MUSTARD LEEKS Heat butter in a medium saucepan over low heat. Add leeks and cook for 3–5 minutes, until softened. Increase to medium-high heat, pour in wine, and cook for 5–10 minutes, until reduced by half. Add cream and cook for another 5 minutes or so, until reduced by a third. Do not boil the mixture. Reduce heat if necessary. Stir in mustard and season with salt and pepper.

PINOT SAUCE Heat butter in a skillet over medium-low heat. Add shallots and sauté for 2–3 minutes, until softened. Add wine and stock and simmer for 5–10 minutes, until reduced by half.

ASSEMBLY Place mustard leeks in the center of each serving plate. Cut phyllo-wrapped packets in half and lay over leeks. Drizzle sauce around plates. Top with a spoonful of tomato jam.

TOMATO JAM

1 Tbsp apple cider vinegar
1 Tbsp brown sugar
Pinch of ground cinnamon
Pinch of ground cloves
Pinch of ground cumin
1 (12-oz) can whole San Marzano
    tomatoes, drained, seeded,
    and chopped
1 Tbsp honey
Kosher salt and black pepper, to taste

PHYLLO-WRAPPED SNAPPER

4 (5-oz) thick snapper fillets
8 slices serrano ham or prosciutto
Bunch of spinach, blanched and
    patted dry
All-purpose flour, for dusting
12 sheets phyllo dough
½ cup (1 stick) butter, melted

MUSTARD LEEKS

1 Tbsp butter
1 leek, white part only, cut into
    2-inch pieces
¼ cup non-oaked white wine
    (preferably Chardonnay)
¾ cup heavy cream
1 Tbsp whole-grain mustard
Kosher salt and black pepper, to taste

PINOT SAUCE

1 tsp butter
1 shallot, thinly sliced
1 cup Pinot Noir
1 cup veal stock (available in soup
    aisles and frozen cases)

Farro, Mushroom, and Kale Salad with Sage–Agave Vinaigrette SERVES 4

This is a light meal on its own. Top it with a protein such as chicken or salmon for a more substantial entrée.

SAGE–AGAVE VINAIGRETTE Combine syrup and sage in a small saucepan over medium heat for 2 minutes. Do not boil. Set aside to cool for 30 minutes.

In a bowl, whisk remaining ingredients. Pour in half of the infused syrup and whisk. Dressing should be slightly sour. Season to taste with more syrup.

SALAD Bring 1⅔ cups water to a boil in a small saucepan, add farro, and cook according to the package directions. Set aside to cool.

Add kale and a drizzle of oil to a large bowl and massage leaves for 30 seconds.

In a medium bowl, combine mushrooms and a little vinaigrette and toss until fully coated. Add kale and farro and toss. Add more vinaigrette as desired.

ASSEMBLY Divide salad equally among 4 plates or place in a large serving bowl or on a platter. Sprinkle with feta and pomegranate seeds. Serve with lemon wedges.

SAGE–AGAVE VINAIGRETTE
½ cup agave syrup
Sprig of sage
½ cup avocado oil
½ cup olive oil
¼ cup lemon juice
1 Tbsp whole-grain mustard
Kosher salt and black pepper, to taste

SALAD
⅔ cup pearled farro
2 cups torn kale leaves
Extra-virgin olive oil, for drizzling
2 cups very thinly sliced white mushrooms (a mandolin works great)
Sage-Agave Vinaigrette (see here)

ASSEMBLY
Salad (see here)
½ cup crumbled feta
½ cup pomegranate seeds
4 lemon wedges, to serve

Bliss

Tony Hernandez

CHEF MARK BLISS cut his teeth working in San Antonio's top kitchens throughout the 1980s and 1990s. When he and his wife, Lisa, chose to open their own doors in 2012, they proved they were ready to make it independently. They reclaimed an old service station in trendy Lavaca, artistically reinventing it as a station for service of the culinary kind.

Chef Bliss's eponymous restaurant embodies the word, focusing on the pleasurable experience of dining. Upscale, contemporary, but never complicated, the seasonal, locally sourced menu has received rave reviews from national travel sites and local and regional reviewers alike. Chef de cuisine Tony Hernandez creates and serves a unique menu that highlights those seasonal ingredients and draws inspiration from culinary capitals spanning from Mexico City to Tokyo. The intimate chef's table is an open window to the center of the action and an immersive experience for devoted food fans.

Meanwhile, general manager Dorian Mills ensures guests at the other intimate indoor tables and on the twinkly outdoor patio are also absorbed in the joy of dining. Bliss has transcended special-occasion dining to become a trusted citywide favorite, thanks to its pursuit of big-city dreams and its ability to deliver on that vision.

Gulf Snapper Crudo SERVES 2

The pleasure of eating this dish is in both the presentation and the refreshingly bright, playful flavors. Red snapper from the Texas Gulf Coast is plentiful in San Antonio during the summer months, but redfish or ahi tuna also works well. Be sure to serve it with a spoon so you don't miss a drop.

CRUDO BROTH Blend all ingredients in a blender.

ASSEMBLY Pour broth into 2 deep black serving bowls. Gently place sliced fish across the center of each bowl. Arrange strawberries and pears across the top of the fish. Garnish with oil and flowers (if using).

Leftover broth can be refrigerated in an airtight container for up to 10 days. It can be used in additional crudo servings.

NOTE >> Koji is a type of Japanese starter where partially cooked rice has been inoculated with a fermentation culture. It's the basis of many familiar Japanese ingredients such as soy sauce, miso, and sake. It is generally available in Asian grocery stores.

CRUDO BROTH
Juice of 5 limes
Juice of 5 oranges
Juice of 3 lemons
1 cup unsweetened coconut milk
½ cup champagne vinegar
2 Tbsp koji (see Note)
Pinch of kosher salt
Pinch of sugar

ASSEMBLY
Crudo Broth (see here)
3 oz Gulf snapper, thinly sliced
2 strawberries, each evenly cut into 4 slices
1 Asian pear, cut into matchsticks
Chili oil, for garnish (optional)
Edible flowers, for garnish (optional)

Charred Octopus over Roasted Baby Yukon Potatoes with Coriander Dressing SERVES 8

Once you've succeeded at cooking octopus, it will surely become a mainstay on your table. Here, tender octopus takes on the flavors of the simmering broth and holds the smokiness of the char beautifully.

OCTOPUS Fill a stockpot with water and add all ingredients except octopus. Bring to a simmer over medium heat.

Rinse octopus and gently lower it into the pot. Simmer, uncovered, for 2 hours, until tender. Never allow the water to come to a rolling boil.

Using tongs, transfer octopus to a wire rack set over a baking sheet and set aside to cool to room temperature. Discard water and vegetables.

CHARRED OCTOPUS Heat oil and butter in a large cast-iron skillet over high heat. Add octopus, turn occasionally, and sear for a minute, or until charred to your liking. Add garlic and thyme and baste octopus with remaining melted butter in the pan.

Transfer octopus to a plate and drizzle with lemon juice.

ROASTED BABY YUKONS Preheat oven to 375°F.

In a bowl, combine all ingredients and toss until potatoes are evenly coated. Transfer potatoes to a baking sheet and roast for 30–45 minutes, until tender and crispy.

CORIANDER DRESSING In a dry skillet, toast coriander seeds over low-medium heat for 2–3 minutes, until fragrant.

Combine coriander seeds and remaining ingredients except oil in a blender. Blend on medium speed, then gradually add oil and blend until the mixture is thick and emulsified. Increase to high speed for 4 seconds. Pour through a fine-mesh sieve into a bowl.

ASSEMBLY Cut the tentacles off the octopus. Place 6–8 pieces of potato in the center of each serving plate. Top each plate with a tentacle, then drizzle coriander dressing on top and garnish with microgreens (if using).

OCTOPUS
4 cloves garlic, peeled
3 sprigs thyme
3 stalks celery
2 white onions
1 carrot
1 shallot
1 Tbsp Spanish paprika
1 Tbsp kosher salt
2–4 lbs whole octopus, head and beak removed and discarded

CHARRED OCTOPUS
2 Tbsp extra-virgin olive oil
2 Tbsp butter
Octopus (see here)
2 cloves garlic, peeled
Sprig of thyme
Juice of 1 lemon

ROASTED BABY YUKONS
1 lb baby Yukon Gold potatoes, unpeeled and halved
¼ cup olive oil
1 clove garlic, minced
Kosher salt (preferably Morton's) and black pepper, to taste

CORIANDER DRESSING
2 Tbsp coriander seeds
2 cloves garlic, minced
1 shallot, finely chopped
½ cup white balsamic vinegar
½ cup honey
¼ cup sherry vinegar
1 Tbsp tamarind paste
½ Tbsp Dijon mustard
1 cup canola oil
Microgreens, for garnish (optional)

Botika
Geronimo Lopez

PERUVIAN–ASIAN FUSION is a marriage made in culinary heaven. And it's nothing new in Peru, where *chifa* (Peruvian-Chinese) and *nikkei* (Peruvian-Japanese) restaurants have proliferated for nearly a century. Botika brings this fun playground to diners who appreciate unique flavors and textural combinations. Venezuela-born chef Geronimo Lopez, who brings his veteran cooking skills and native Caribbean flair to the yard, adds even more frivolity.

Lopez spent some of his career at Four Seasons resorts worldwide before settling in as the opening chef-instructor for The Culinary Institute of America's student-run restaurant at Pearl. The move to open Botika freed him to create a vibrant menu and a colorful décor where he channels his adventurous spirit into the food and cocktails that tell the "how we met" story of Peru's melded cuisine.

When soy and ginger join hot peppers and sweet potatoes, they romp with wild abandon, cutting out a new niche of enchanting flavors that work well together. Start with a round of sushi rolls accented with quinoa or Peruvian rocoto peppers, then follow up with a fried rice sprinkled with corn. And don't pass up the yakisoba noodles with pickled peppers or crispy fries with olives and queso fresco. Every course will sing its harmonious song, in its native languages, as you join in.

BOTIKA Crispy Cebiche Dos Texturas, p. 44 and Aeropuerto Chaufa Rice, p. 45

Crispy Cebiche Dos Texturas SERVES 4–6

Leche de tigre, or tiger's milk, differentiates Peruvian cebiche from Mexican ceviche, adding a tangy and fruity kick to raw fish and seafood. Lightly grilled pineapple and mellow roasted sweet potatoes round out the unique flavor, reinforcing the authenticity of its Peruvian roots.

TIGER'S MILK

1 cup chopped sole, flounder, or snapper
1 cup chopped fresh pineapple
½ stalk celery, sliced
½ cup red onion, thinly sliced
¼ cup lightly packed cilantro leaves
¼ cup roughly chopped ginger
2 cloves garlic, minced
1 habanero pepper, seeded and finely chopped
1 cup lime juice
Kosher salt and white pepper, to taste

MARINATED SHRIMP

½ batch Tiger's Milk (see here)
1 lb shrimp, peeled, deveined, and poached

FRIED FISH

Peanut oil, for deep-frying
Cornstarch or rice starch, for dredging
Kosher salt and white pepper
1 lb white fish fillets such as sole, flounder, or snapper, sliced into 1-inch squares

ASSEMBLY

2 sweet potatoes, scrubbed
¼ whole pineapple
½ head Bibb or Boston lettuce, leaves separated
Marinated Shrimp (see here)
Fried Fish (see here)
½ batch Tiger's Milk (see here)
Cilantro leaves, for garnish
1 red bird's eye chile, seeded and very thinly sliced, for garnish
1 scallion, thinly sliced, for garnish
Togarashi, for sprinkling

TIGER'S MILK In a chilled bowl, mix all ingredients except salt and pepper. Season with salt and pepper, cover, and refrigerate for at least 2 hours or overnight.

Using a mortar and pestle, grind the mixture. Strain through a fine-mesh sieve and reserve liquid. Discard solids.

MARINATED SHRIMP Combine tiger's milk and shrimp in a bowl and marinate in the refrigerator for at least 15 minutes.

FRIED FISH Heat oil in a deep fryer or deep saucepan over medium-high heat until the temperature reaches 350°F–375°F.

Place cornstarch (or rice starch) in a shallow bowl. Lightly sprinkle salt and pepper over fish, then dip the fish pieces into starch.

Working in batches to avoid overcrowding and averting your face from the hot oil, gently lower fish into the deep fryer and deep-fry for 2–3 minutes, until golden brown. Using a slotted spoon, transfer fish to a paper towel–lined plate to drain. Set aside.

ASSEMBLY Chill a large serving bowl.

Preheat oven to 350°F.

Roast sweet potatoes for 45 minutes, until softened. When cool enough to handle, remove skin and cut flesh into ½-inch cubes. Set aside to cool completely.

Preheat a grill or grill pan over high heat.

Add pineapple to the grill and sear on each side for 3 minutes. Transfer to a cutting board. When cool enough to handle, cut into ½-inch cubes.

Combine sweet potatoes and pineapple in the chilled bowl. Arrange lettuce leaves around the side of the bowl. Add shrimp and fish to the center. Ladle enough tiger's milk to just cover fish but do not drown fish in the liquid. Garnish with cilantro, chile, and scallions. Sprinkle togarashi on top.

Serve with a spoon, using the lettuce leaves as cups or wraps.

Aeropuerto Chaufa Rice SERVES 4-6

The word *aeropuerto* in this dish has nothing to do with an airport. It simply refers to the fact that everything lands in the bowl of this homestyle fried rice that is *puro chifa* (Peruvian-Chinese) cuisine.

Preheat a grill or a grill pan over medium-high heat.

Season chicken and shrimp with salt and pepper. Add chicken to the grill and cook for 5 minutes. Flip and cook another 5 minutes.

Meanwhile, add shrimp to the grill and cook for 2–3 minutes. Flip and cook for another 2–3 minutes, until cooked through. (The chicken and shrimp should be seared on both sides.) Transfer chicken and shrimp to a cutting board. Slice chicken and cut shrimp in half. Transfer both to a plate and set aside.

Heat 2 tablespoons peanut (or vegetable) oil in a wok or large skillet over high heat. Add eggs and cook for 1–1½ minutes, untouched, until sides are set. Carefully flip the omelet over and cook for another 2 minutes. Transfer to a cutting board, then cut into strips or cubes. Set aside.

In the same wok, heat remaining 2 tablespoons peanut (or vegetable) oil over high heat. Add garlic and ginger and stir for 1 minute, until fragrant. Add peas, bell peppers, onions, and carrots and stir-fry for 1 minute. Add rice and stir-fry for 2–3 minutes, breaking up any clumps with a wooden spoon. Mix well with the vegetables. Stir in chicken, shrimp, and sausage. Add soy sauce (or tamari) and vinegar.

Remove the wok from the heat, stir in sesame oil, and set aside for 4 minutes for flavors to mingle. Transfer the mixture to a large serving platter and top with egg, scallions, and herbs. Garnish with pineapple and peanuts (if using).

NOTE >> *Lap cheong* is a type of sweet, air-dried Cantonese sausage made with pork and pork lard. Generally, it's steamed (try it with plain white rice) or stir-fried with other ingredients. *Pinoy* is a Filipino spicy coconut vinegar. Both are available in Asian grocery stores.

The word *chaufa* roughly translates in Chinese to "fried rice," a quintessential dish on *chifa* menus.

2 boneless, skinless chicken thighs

2 cups medium shrimp, peeled and deveined

Kosher salt and white pepper

¼ cup peanut or vegetable oil (divided)

3 eggs, lightly beaten

2 cloves garlic, minced

1 Tbsp grated ginger

¾ cup sugar snap peas, cut diagonally

½ red bell pepper, seeded, deveined, and diced (½ cup)

1 small red onion, thinly sliced (½ cup)

½ carrot, coarsely grated (½ cup)

3 cups day-old cooked short-grain rice

1–2 Chinese sausages (lap cheong), chopped (½ cup) (see Note)

6 Tbsp soy sauce or tamari

2 Tbsp Filipino coconut vinegar (pinoy) or apple cider vinegar (see Note)

2 tsp sesame oil

3–5 scallions, thinly sliced (1 cup)

Fresh herbs such as cilantro, Thai basil, or mint, to taste

1 cup diced pineapple, for garnish

1 cup peanuts, toasted and finely chopped, for garnish (optional)

Brasserie
Mon Chou Chou

Jeff Balfour (R)
and Laurent Réa (L)

A TRANSFORMATION takes place when you walk through the doors of Mon Chou Chou. You're in Paris, you're dazzled, and you're excited about dining. That immersive experience emanates from experienced restaurateurs who gathered San Antonio's top French chef, Laurent Réa, most hospitable maître d', Philippe Placé (also French), and savviest marketing guru, Jérôme Sérot (yup, French), then gave them the reins to make magic happen. Placé and Sérot are principal partners in the Southerleigh Hospitality Group, which owns the brasserie, so for them, this passion project is both good business and good for the soul.

The restaurant opened during the dark days of December 2020, and the all-day menu tells the story of culinary prowess through regional French comfort food that lights up the city with hopeful glee. Dishes include the Lyonnaise onion soup with Emmental and cognac, frisée salad topped with warm goat cheese and herbes de Provence, classic beef bourguignon, thick double lamb chops with bordelaise sauce, and an Alsatian-style braised red cabbage. It's a culinary tour on a table that's also a tour de force. And no meal would be complete without an order of the raclette cheese sandwich, a decadent tableside starter that has melted cheese scraped from the wheel onto a split baguette. It became an immediate Instagram star.

BRASSERIE MON CHOU CHOU Provençal Monkfish with Confit Potatoes, p. 48

Provençal Monkfish with Confit Potatoes SERVES 6

This classic family-style entrée, a regular feature on the brasserie menu, is perfect with a simple side salad, crusty bread and butter, and olives.

CONFIT POTATOES

1 (1½-lb) bag fingerling or marble potatoes

6 cloves garlic, peeled

3 sprigs thyme

Kosher salt and black pepper

2 cups olive oil, plus extra if needed

PROVENÇAL SAUCE

2 Tbsp olive oil

1 onion, sliced

1 (32-oz) can crushed San Marzano tomatoes

12 oz mixed Mediterranean olives, pitted

MONKFISH

2 Tbsp vegetable oil

3 lbs monkfish tails, membranes removed

3 Tbsp all-purpose flour

Kosher salt and black pepper

2 Tbsp butter

Confit Potatoes (see here)

BUTTER SAUCE

1 Tbsp olive oil

2 shallots, chopped

¼ cup dry white wine

½ cup heavy cream

¼ cup (½ stick) butter

Kosher salt and black pepper, to taste

ASSEMBLY

Chopped Italian parsley, for garnish

CONFIT POTATOES Preheat oven to 350°F.

In a large bowl, combine potatoes, garlic, and thyme. Season with salt and pepper.

Arrange in a snug single layer in a lidded ovenproof Dutch oven, at least 5 inches deep. Pour in enough oil to cover potatoes. Cover with lid and wrap the entire dish in aluminum foil to seal. Bake for 1½ hours.

Using a slotted spoon, transfer potatoes to a bowl and set aside. Leftover oil can be filtered and reserved for another use.

PROVENÇAL SAUCE Heat oil in a medium saucepan over medium heat. Add onions and sauté for 5–6 minutes, until translucent. Add tomatoes and olives, reduce to medium-low heat, and simmer for 10 minutes, until reduced and thickened. Set aside and keep warm.

MONKFISH Heat oil in a large skillet over high heat. Place monkfish on a plate and dust with flour. Season with salt and pepper. Averting your face from the hot oil, carefully add fish to the skillet and cook for 3 minutes on each side until golden brown (see Note). Reduce heat to low and add butter. Spoon butter over fish for 2 minutes. Add potatoes and cook for 3 minutes, until potatoes are golden brown. Set aside and keep warm.

NOTE >> When cooking monkfish, the rule of thumb is to cook it for 6 minutes per side for every inch of thickness. Overcooking will cause it to become rubbery. Allow monkfish to rest for 2 minutes before serving.

BUTTER SAUCE Combine oil and shallots in a small saucepan over medium-low heat. Add wine and gently simmer until reduced by half. Add cream and simmer for another 2–3 minutes, until the mixture starts to thicken and is reduced by another half. Whisk in butter. Strain sauce through a fine-mesh sieve. Season with salt and pepper.

ASSEMBLY Place Provençal sauce in the center of each serving bowl. Lay fish on top and arrange potatoes around fish. Spoon butter sauce over fish and garnish with parsley.

Mocha Pot de Crème SERVES 8

This rich, creamy, and sinfully satisfying "pudding" is dessert and coffee in a single dish.

Preheat oven to 300°F.

In a medium saucepan, combine milk, cream, coffee, and vanilla over medium heat. Whisk in chocolate and stir until melted.

In a medium bowl, whisk egg yolks and sugar. Add 3 tablespoons of the warm milk mixture and whisk to temper the yolks. Slowly whisk the yolk mixture into the milk, until thickened and temperature reaches 175°F. Strain through a fine-mesh sieve.

Pour mixture into 8 (5-ounce) ramekins. Fill a roasting pan with water, about 1 inch deep. Add ramekins to the pan and bake for 30 minutes.

Carefully transfer ramekins to a rack and cool at room temperature for 30 minutes. Refrigerate at least 1 hour.

To serve, top with a dollop of whipped cream. Cover and refrigerate any leftover pots de crème for up to 3 days.

2 cups whole milk
1 cup heavy cream
2 shots hot espresso coffee
2¼ tsp vanilla extract
10 oz dark chocolate (55% cacao)
9 egg yolks
¼ cup sugar
Whipped cream, to serve

Bunz Handcrafted Burgers

Thierry Burkle (R)
and Edwin Salazar (L)

AFTER FORTY years of owning and operating two of the city's leading continental restaurants, L'Etoile and The Grill at Leon Springs, Thierry Burkle has made a sharp turn to the fast-casual Bunz Hand-crafted Burgers, situated on a prime corner along downtown's Houston Street.

Burkle's culinary career began in his native Paris and took him to Washington, D.C., before he settled in San Antonio. His business partner in this venture, Edwin Salazar, the former sous chef at The Grill, grew up between El Paso and Chihuahua, Mexico. He completed his culinary education in Italy, then staged in upscale kitchens across the globe, before landing at The Grill. The duo infuses Bunz with fine-dining techniques (house-made brioche buns, sauces, pickles, and patties) and attention to proportion and aesthetics. The locally milled specialty flour in the buns, the daily grind of beef in the burgers, and the imaginative toppings—such as Asian BBQ ribs and fresh pear slices—make for fun twists on an all-American classic. But it's more than just your standard burger fare at this downtown burger bastion. Skillfully prepared seafood dishes include a jumbo crab cake "burger" that's nearly all crab and no cake.

Bunz opened as the pandemic shut down the city, yet it found a strong following through takeout and delivery. And when it comes to dining options, it's becoming a buzzy breakfast destination, a hopping lunchtime café, and a new dinner joint for locals in the know. Rightfully so.

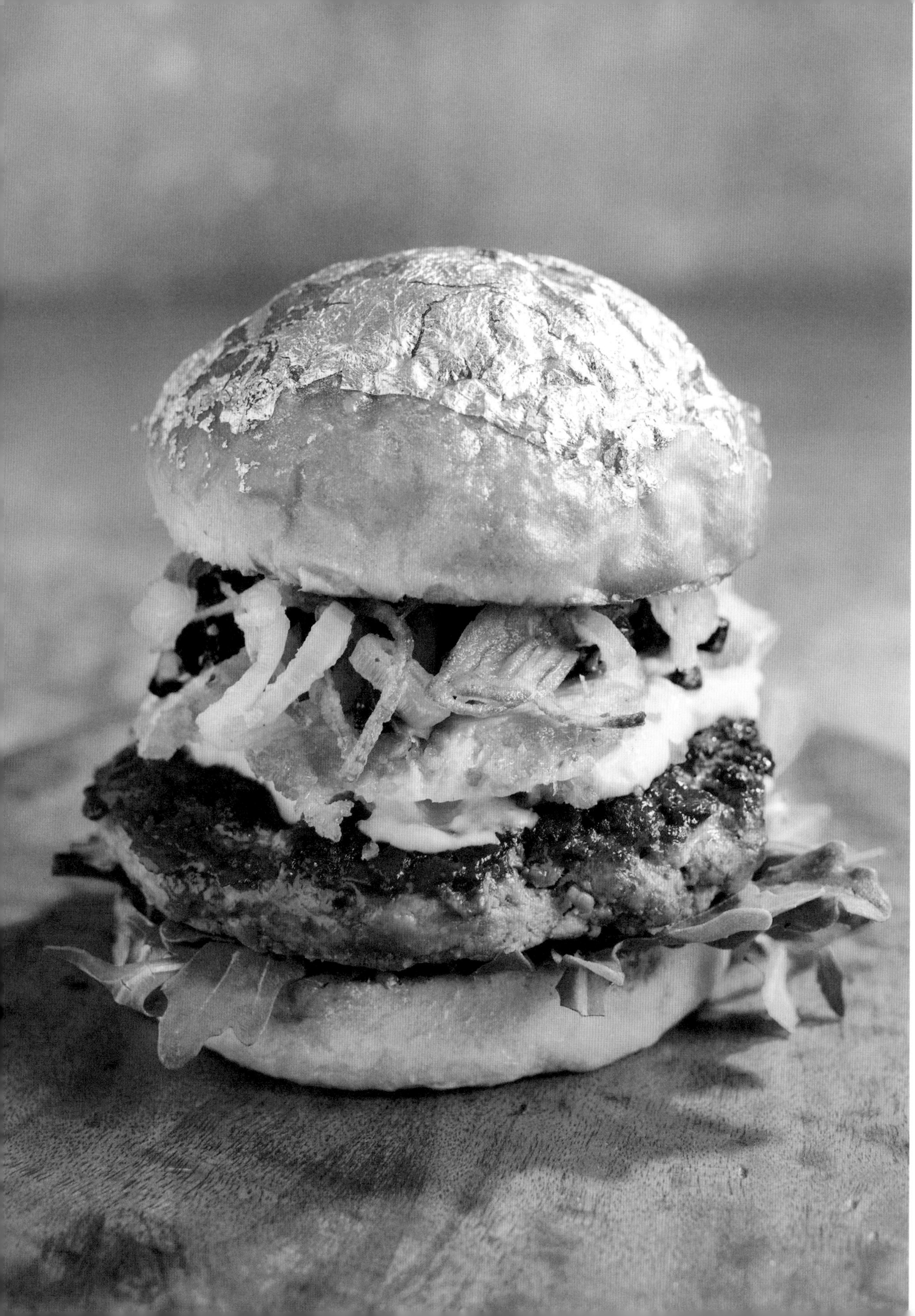

 Golden Bunz Burger, p. 54

Tasty Bunz Brioche SERVES 8

In a stand mixer fitted with the hook attachment, combine yeast, sugar, milk, egg yolk, and 3 tablespoons + 1 teaspoon water. Using a fork or whisk, mix gently by hand. Set aside for 15 minutes to ferment and foam.

Set the mixer to medium-low speed. Slowly add flour and salt to the yeast mixture, until flour is incorporated. Add butter, a bit at a time, until the dough is tacky.

Grease a large bowl or container with oil and add the dough. Cover with plastic wrap and set aside at room temperature to rise for 1 hour.

Preheat oven to 350°F. Line a baking sheet with parchment paper and grease the paper with oil.

Using your fist, punch down the center of the dough. Portion dough into 8 equal pieces and shape them into balls. Place on the baking sheet.

Beat egg white in a small bowl. Brush the top of each dough ball with egg white, then sprinkle sesame (or poppy) seeds on top (if using). Cover and rest the dough at room temperature for 25 minutes, until rounds are 5 inches in diameter.

Bake for 5 minutes. Rotate the baking sheet and bake for another 5 minutes, until golden brown. Once buns have cooled to room temperature, dress the top of each with a sheet of gold leaf (if using).

1 (7-g) packet active dry yeast
2 Tbsp + ¾ tsp sugar
½ cup whole milk, warmed to 100°F
1 egg, separated
2 cups all-purpose flour
1 tsp sea salt
3 Tbsp softened butter
Vegetable oil, for greasing
Sesame or poppy seeds, for sprinkling (optional)
8 sheets edible 24-karat gold leaf (optional)

Golden Bunz Burger SERVES 2

BLACK GARLIC AND CHILI FLAKE AIOLI

2 egg yolks

Pinch of salt

Pinch of white pepper

1 Tbsp apple cider vinegar

6 cloves Texas Black Gold garlic, peeled

1 Tbsp chili flakes

1 cup corn oil

DIJON GOUDA FONDUE

2 Tbsp Dijon mustard

⅓ cup heavy cream

8 oz Gouda cheese, shredded

1 tsp Worcestershire sauce

CRISPY SWEETBREADS

5 oz fresh sweetbreads, about ½ medium lobe

1 medium carrot, roughly chopped

1 stalk celery, roughly chopped

½ small white onion, roughly chopped

½ cup heavy cream, less or more as needed

½ cup chicken broth, less or more as needed

2 Tbsp Dijon mustard

½ cup unseasoned panko breadcrumbs

2 Tbsp cooking oil

BLACK GARLIC AND CHILI FLAKE AIOLI Using a blender or an immersion blender in a large bowl, combine all ingredients except oil. With the motor running, slowly drizzle in oil until the mixture has emulsified to the consistency of mayonnaise. If the mixture is too thick, add a splash of water. Unused aioli can be refrigerated in a sealed container for up to a week.

DIJON GOUDA FONDUE Combine mustard and cream in a medium saucepan and bring to a low simmer over medium-low heat. Add cheese and slowly allow it to melt, stirring often to prevent sticking. Once cheese has melted, stir in Worcestershire and continue to cook for 10–15 minutes to combine flavors. The finished sauce should be smooth and gooey.

CRISPY SWEETBREADS Inspect sweetbreads and discard any stringy membranes. Place sweetbreads, carrots, celery, and onions in a medium saucepan. Just cover with equal amounts of cream and broth. Bring to a simmer for 40–50 minutes, until tender. Remove sweetbreads from liquid and allow to come to room temperature. Discard liquid and vegetables.

Cut sweetbreads into ¼-inch-thick slices. Place mustard in a small bowl and breadcrumbs in another small bowl. Lightly coat each slice of sweetbread in mustard, then in breadcrumbs.

Heat a frying pan over medium heat and add oil. Cook coated slices of sweetbreads until golden brown on each side. Place on a paper towel to drain.

MUSHROOM DUXELLES Heat a large skillet over medium-high heat. Add butter and swirl to coat the surface of the pan. Add shallots, garlic, and mushrooms and cook over medium heat, stirring frequently to encourage liquids to evaporate, about 5 minutes. The mixture should release its liquids and mushrooms should appear dry and brown. Remove from heat and stir in salt and pepper. Set aside.

CARAMELIZED SHALLOTS Heat a large skillet over medium heat and add oil. Stir in shallots and cook slowly over medium-low heat for 20–30 minutes, until soft and brown. Stir often to avoid burning and reduce heat if shallots appear to blacken.

BURGERS Divide beef in half and form equal patties. Put on a plate, cover, and refrigerate until ready to prepare.

Preheat a grill pan to medium-high for 5 minutes. (This will ensure the meat sears on the outside and remains juicy.)

Remove patties from the refrigerator. Lightly season both sides with salt. Add patties to the grill and cook for 4 minutes. Be patient and don't move the patties until you're ready to flip them to the other side. Cook for another 4 minutes to achieve a slightly pink center.

ASSEMBLY Toast buns to your preference. (This prevents moisture from penetrating the bun.)

Spread a thin layer of aioli on each of the bottom buns. Top with arugula, burger patty, fondue, sweetbreads, mushrooms, and shallots. Spread fig marmalade on the cut side of the top bun and place on top.

Serve immediately.

MUSHROOM DUXELLES
1 Tbsp butter
1 medium shallot, finely diced
1 garlic clove, minced
20 large white mushrooms, finely chopped
½ tsp salt
½ tsp white pepper

CARAMELIZED SHALLOTS
1 Tbsp olive oil
10 medium shallots, cut into thin slices (1 cup)

BURGERS
1 lb 80/20 ground beef
Salt

ASSEMBLY
2 buns from Tasty Bunz Brioche (see page 53)
Black Garlic and Chili Flake Aioli (see here)
2 handfuls arugula leaves
Burgers (see here)
Dijon Gouda Fondue (see here)
Crispy Sweetbreads (see here)
Mushroom Duxelles (see here)
Caramelized Shallots (see here)
2 Tbsp store-bought fig marmalade

Cabernet Grill
Texas Wine Country
Restaurant

Ross Burtwell

EXECUTIVE CHEF Ross Burtwell's restaurant holds the distinction of being the first in the state to feature an all-Texas wine list. Two decades later, Cabernet Grill continues to offer the widest selection of Texas wines of any restaurant in the nation, boasting more than 180 wines at any given time. That wine lover's draw was quickly eclipsed by the quality food coming from the kitchen, a celebration of the Hill Country's culinary roots. The packed as-Texas-as-possible menu includes artisanal goat cheese, Hill Country pecans and peaches, farm-fresh veggies, and garden herbs. Diners are tempted by wild-caught Texas Gulf shrimp, locally raised quail, and an over-the-top chicken-fried rib-eye topped with lobster and green chile cream gravy that screams "I'm in Texas."

The setting makes the same geographical statement. Just past the bubbling water feature, off the wood-planked porch, are paths to Cotton Gin Village—a quaint bed-and-breakfast composed of rustic cabins decorated with high-end furnishings and luxurious finishes. You don't need to lodge in one of the cabins to enjoy a Cabernet Grill meal, but I would certainly recommend it to experience true Texas Hill Country hospitality, charm, and chill.

Cotton Gin Village Granola

MAKES 3 1/2 LBS

A stay at the rustic-chic cabins of Cotton Gin Village now includes a hot breakfast basket delivered daily to each cabin. But in the early years of the B&B, chef Burtwell and his team stocked the cabins with fruit, yogurt, and this hearty house-made granola.

WET MIX In a small saucepan, combine all ingredients over medium heat. Stir and bring to a simmer. Remove the saucepan from heat, then set aside to cool until warm (but not hot) to the touch.

DRY MIX In a large bowl, mix all ingredients.

ASSEMBLY Preheat oven to 350°F. Line 3 baking sheets with parchment paper.

Pour wet mix into dry mix. Using your hands (you can wear disposable gloves if needed), evenly disperse the coating and eliminate the large lumps as you mix. (The wet mix will be quite warm—take care not to burn yourself.)

Pour thin layers of the mixture onto the prepared baking sheets. Bake for 10 minutes. Stir granola, then bake for another 5–10 minutes or until evenly and lightly toasted. Set aside to cool.

Distribute dried fruit evenly among the baking sheets. Granola can be stored in quart-size canning jars or zip-top bags for up to 3 months.

WET MIX

6 Tbsp butter
1 tsp ground cinnamon
1 tsp five-spice powder
½ cup brown sugar
¼ cup honey
½ tsp kosher salt

DRY MIX

9 oz cornflakes
3 cups rolled oats
1 cup unsweetened shredded coconut
½ cup white sesame seeds
½ cup sliced almonds
½ cup sunflower seeds
½ cup pepitas
½ cup walnut pieces

ASSEMBLY

Wet Mix (see here)
Dry Mix (see here)
3 cups mixed dried fruit such as raisins, golden raisins, currants, cranberries, peaches, pineapple, and papaya

Texas Twinkies
with Jezebel Sauce SERVES 4–6

According to chef Ross Burtwell, this dish is by far the most popular appetizer at Cabernet Grill. "Our kitchen staff struggles to keep up with the demand, especially on busy weekends. We use our own house-made beer sausage, but fresh raw bratwurst, breakfast sausage, or even a good-quality chorizo will work."

TEXAS TWINKIES Preheat oven to 400°F.

Lay jalapeños, cut side up, on a baking sheet. Slice cheese into 12 matchsticks, about ¼-inch wide and 2 inches long (so that they fit into the jalapeño halves). Dust cheese with Cajun seasoning. Place a piece of cheese in each jalapeño.

Place a piece of sausage over each jalapeño. Using your fingers, mold sausage over jalapeño until all the cheese has been covered.

Wrap each jalapeño in a slice of bacon, starting at one end and spiraling it to the other end. If necessary, trim the bacon to size. Bake for 15 minutes, until bacon is browned and sausage is cooked through.

JEZEBEL SAUCE Combine all ingredients in a small bowl and mix well. Garnish with chili threads and parsley (if using).

ASSEMBLY Transfer Texas Twinkies to a serving platter and serve immediately with Jezebel sauce.

TEXAS TWINKIES
6 large jalapeño peppers, halved
  lengthwise, seeded, and deveined
2½ oz extra-sharp white cheddar
1 tsp Cajun seasoning
12 oz raw pork sausage, divided into
  12 pieces
12 thin slices bacon

JEZEBEL SAUCE
1 cup mayonnaise
¼ cup orange marmalade
¼ cup prepared horseradish
1 tsp Tabasco sauce
½ tsp kosher salt
Pinch of black pepper
Chili threads, for garnish (optional)
Chopped parsley, for garnish
  (optional)

Camp Outpost
Matthew Betlach

WOOD-FIRE COOKING goes to glamping heights at this casual American spot with a camping theme. Housed in a former warehouse, decked-out Camp Outpost has a new, spacious patio with picnic tables and a vintage Airstream that serves as a bar and merch store. Order inside from a compact yet seasonally changing menu of rotisserie meats, entrée salads, tacos, sandwiches, burgers, and sides, and soon, a happy camper will bring a metal tray of your items to your table. This is one of the first Camp Outposts being staked around the country, all with the same concept of upscale open-fire rotisserie fare and regionally nuanced menus.

Chef Matthew Betlach, who oversees the San Antonio location, adds a local San Antonio spin to the dishes. Moist wood-fire rotisserie chicken, tri-tip steak, and baby back ribs with creamy cheddar grits are a giant leap beyond traditional campfire meals. So is a standout slow-roasted pork sandwich that was never conceived to be subtle, topped with a slew of cabbage slaw and fried jalapeños. The generously portioned fried brussels

sprouts, served with a sweetly spiced honey-mustard dipping sauce, are designed for sharing. And in a nod to the city's history, the harmonious Mission Salad balances crisp romaine with roasted corn, black beans, avocado, queso fresco, and tortilla chips—all coated in a light guajillo-ranch dressing. Beer, wine, ciders, and batched tap cocktails, including a vodka-laced hard tea, make Camp Outpost a fun adult camping trip. Kids are welcome, too.

 Blackened Redfish with Charred Tomatoes and Corn Relish, p. 62

Blackened Redfish with Charred Tomatoes and Corn Relish SERVES 6

Making your own blackening spice is easy and gives you control over the intensity of the heat. If you prefer, use jarred blackening spice, available in the spice aisle of most grocery stores.

CORN RELISH
1 large ear corn, husk and
    silk removed
2 Tbsp olive oil
1 large red bell pepper
½ cup crumbled queso fresco cheese,
    cotija cheese, farmer's cheese,
    or feta
Bunch of cilantro, roughly chopped
Zest and juice of 2 limes
Kosher salt and black pepper, to taste

BLACKENING SPICE
1 Tbsp garlic powder
1 Tbsp onion powder
1 Tbsp smoked paprika
1 Tbsp chili powder
1 Tbsp dried thyme
1 tsp kosher salt
1 tsp cayenne powder

CHARRED TOMATOES
2 Tbsp olive oil
4 large heirloom tomatoes, sliced
    horizontally into 3 thick slices,
    each ¾–1-inch thick
Kosher salt and black pepper

BLACKENED REDFISH
6 redfish fillets, ½-inch thick
    (2½ lbs total)
Premade or homemade
    Blackening Spice (see here)
1 tsp olive oil, for brushing

ASSEMBLY
2 limes, cut into wedges

CORN RELISH Preheat a grill or grill pan over medium-high heat.

Brush corn lightly with oil. Add corn to the grill and char on all sides for 5 minutes total. Set aside to cool, then slice kernels off the cob.

In the same pan over medium-high heat, add bell pepper and char on all sides for 5–7 minutes total, until skin is blackened and blistered. Place pepper in a covered container for 10 minutes. Peel skin, then remove seeds and veins. Dice pepper to the same size as corn kernels.

In a small bowl, combine corn, bell peppers, cheese, cilantro, and lime zest and juice. Season with salt and pepper. Set aside.

BLACKENING SPICE Mix all ingredients in a small bowl. Leftover blackening spice can be stored in an airtight container for up to 2 months.

CHARRED TOMATOES Heat a cast-iron skillet over medium-high heat. Drizzle oil over tomatoes, then season with salt and pepper. Add tomatoes to the skillet and char for 1–2 minutes, untouched. Flip over and char for another 1–2 minutes. (If tomatoes stick to the skillet, they're not ready to be flipped.) Set charred tomatoes on a cooling rack over a drip pan.

BLACKENED REDFISH Sprinkle fillets with blackening spice. Wipe the skillet used for the tomatoes, then brush the bottom with oil. Preheat over high heat.

Working in batches to avoid overcrowding, add fish and fry for 3–4 minutes. Flip over and fry for another 3–4 minutes. Transfer fillets to a plate or baking sheet.

ASSEMBLY Shingle 2 slices charred tomatoes on each plate, then lay a fillet on top, or serve family style on a platter with fillets on top of tomatoes. Garnish each fillet with 2 tablespoons corn relish. Serve with lime wedges.

Baked Stuffed Apples SERVES 6

This simple, gluten-free dessert tastes like crustless apple pie.

FILLING Combine all ingredients in a bowl and mix well.

BAKED STUFFED APPLES Preheat oven to 400°F.

Slice off a bit of the bottom ridge of each apple so it stands upright. Cut off ¼ inch from stem end to create a flat top. Using a paring knife, carefully core apple three-quarters of the way down and remove seeds. You will have a hollow apple with a ½-inch-thick base. (The goal is to remove enough flesh to hold the filling, but not so much that the structure is weakened.) Repeat with remaining apples.

Pack apples with filling. Add a little more to create a dome that will cover any exposed apple flesh. Place apples in a 9- x 12-inch baking pan. Add 1 inch of water, then cover with aluminum foil. Bake for 20 minutes, until apples are soft but not collapsed. Set aside to cool to room temperature.

ASSEMBLY Place an apple on its side on an individual plate. Slice in half to expose the filling. Top with a scoop of ice cream and a drizzle of warm caramel sauce. Repeat with remaining apples.

NOTE >> If not serving immediately, cover and refrigerate whole baked apples. When ready to serve, simply cover with aluminum foil and reheat in a 350°F oven for 10 minutes.

FILLING
2 cups rolled oats
1 cup brown sugar
½ cup sliced almonds
½ cup chopped pecans
1 Tbsp ground cinnamon
Pinch of kosher salt
1 cup (2 sticks) butter, melted

BAKED STUFFED APPLES
6 large firm red apples (preferably Honeycrisp or Pink Lady)
Filling (see here)

ASSEMBLY
Baked Stuffed Apples (see here)
Your favorite ice cream, to serve
Store-bought caramel sauce, warmed, to serve

Cappy's

Cappy Lawton (R) *and Trevor Lawton* (L)

IF SUCCESSFUL longevity is a mark of victory, Cappy's has earned pure platinum. Since 1977, this neighborhood gathering place has been serving Texas cuisine to San Antonio's in-the-know crowd. Cappy's is run by the family-owned-and-operated Lawton Restaurant Group, helmed by Cappy and Suzy Lawton and their son Trevor. Cappy himself has become somewhat of a legend, having developed and designed dozens of restaurants over the years across the state.

The menu of this headlining Alamo Heights restaurant reflects Cappy and Suzy's love of food. They seek out culinary inspiration around the world and constantly collect recipes from their intrepid travel adventures. Their chefs source as much produce as they can from local farms.

Signature dishes include char-grilled oysters served in a pool of spicy soy butter, and a burger topped with mashed black beans and crumbled corn chips. Oh, and that cinnamon-spiked chocolate cake? Also legendary, thanks to a family heirloom recipe.

In the kitchen are long-term chefs Gabriel Ibarra, who oversees the culinary activities for the entire restaurant group, and Kris Gribble, who has worked his way into this position over nearly twenty years. It all comes together into a pleasant, reliable, and quality-driven restaurant where generation upon generation of regulars return week after week.

CAPPY's Chilled Zucchini and Roasted Poblano Soup, p. 67 and Pan-Roasted Chicken with Mixed Vegetables, p. 68

Chilled Zucchini and Roasted Poblano Soup SERVES 6–8

ROASTED POBLANO Preheat oven to 400°F.

Roast poblanos in the oven for 25–30 minutes, rotating occasionally, until skins are charred. Transfer peppers to a plastic bag or a bowl and cover. Set aside for 15 minutes to cool, then peel, seed, and coarsely chop. Set aside.

ZUCCHINI AND ROASTED POBLANO SOUP Melt butter in a large saucepan over medium heat. Add onion and sauté for 5–10 minutes, until slightly caramelized.

Add zucchini and stock and bring to a boil over high heat. Reduce to low heat and simmer for 10–15 minutes, until zucchini is fork tender.

Remove from heat and stir in sugar to dissolve. Transfer the mixture to a blender, and add remaining ingredients. Purée until smooth. Season with more salt and pepper.

Transfer the mixture to a bowl and set aside to cool to room temperature. Cover and chill in the refrigerator for at least 2 hours.

ASSEMBLY Taste the chilled soup and season with salt and pepper to taste. Pour into chilled glasses or small bowls. Finish with a pinch of lime zest and a squeeze of lime juice.

ROASTED POBLANO
1–2 poblano peppers

ZUCCHINI AND ROASTED POBLANO SOUP
3 Tbsp butter
1 large onion, roughly chopped
4–5 zucchini, roughly chopped (4 cups)
2 cups chicken stock
¼ tsp sugar
Roasted Poblano (see here)
1 cup half-and-half, plus extra if needed
1 tsp kosher salt, plus extra to taste
1 tsp black pepper, plus extra to taste
½ tsp freshly grated nutmeg
¼ tsp cayenne pepper

ASSEMBLY
Zucchini and Roasted Poblano Soup (see here)
Kosher salt and black pepper
Zest and juice of 1 lime

Pan-Roasted Chicken with Mixed Vegetables SERVES 2–4

There are few more perfect meals than roast chicken and vegetables. In this elevated take on comfort food, the poultry is brined for guaranteed succulence and then pan-roasted to perfection.

PAN-ROASTED CHICKEN

2 Tbsp kosher salt

2 Tbsp brown sugar

2 cloves garlic, peeled and
   lightly crushed

5 black peppercorns, crushed

1 fresh bay leaf, crushed

1 (4-lb) whole organic chicken,
   quartered

1 tsp black pepper

1 Tbsp canola or any neutral oil

10 cherry tomatoes

PAN-ROASTED CHICKEN SAUCE

3 cups low- or no-sodium
   chicken stock

½ cup red wine vinegar

PAN-ROASTED CHICKEN In a large bowl, combine salt, sugar, garlic, peppercorns, bay leaf, and 2 cups cold water. Mix thoroughly to dissolve sugar and salt.

Place chicken and brine in a large sealed bag or container and refrigerate for at least 3 hours, but no more than 24 hours.

Preheat oven to 350°F.

Remove chicken from brine and pat dry with a paper towel. Season with black pepper. Heat oil in a large ovenproof cast-iron skillet over high heat, until oil begins to ripple. Averting your face from the hot oil, carefully arrange chicken in the skillet, flesh side down. (It seems counterintuitive if you're accustomed to searing the skin side first, but this is correct!) Sear for 5 minutes, until browned. Flip the chicken over and remove the skillet from the heat.

Arrange tomatoes around chicken, place the skillet in the oven, and roast for 30–45 minutes, until the thickest part of the chicken reaches an internal temperature of 170°F. Set aside, uncovered, to rest.

PAN-ROASTED CHICKEN SAUCE Combine stock and vinegar in a medium saucepan over medium heat. Bring to a boil, then reduce to medium-low heat and simmer for 30 minutes, until ½ cup of liquid remains. Set aside.

ROASTED VEGETABLES Preheat oven to 350°F.

Cut fennel in half from stem to root. Lay flat on a cutting board and thinly slice into ⅛-inch strips. Set aside. Rinse red beets, golden beets, and carrots.

Transfer veggies to a baking sheet. Rub lightly with oil and season with salt and pepper. Roast for 30 minutes, until fork tender. Set aside to cool, then peel and cut beets and carrots into ⅛-inch-thick slices.

Bring a medium saucepan of water to a boil. Add snow peas and cook for 1–2 minutes. (Peas should still be crispy.) Using a slotted spoon, transfer peas to a bowl of ice water and chill. Drain, then slice diagonally in half. Place all the prepared vegetables on a baking sheet and set aside.

ASSEMBLY Mix butter into chicken sauce and heat until warmed through.

Place vegetables in the center of a serving dish. Top with dark meat, then white. Drizzle sauce on top, then artfully arrange tomatoes on the plate. Enjoy!

ROASTED VEGETABLES

2 fennel bulbs, tops and ends trimmed
2 red beets
2 golden beets
2 carrots
Olive oil, for rubbing
Kosher salt and black pepper
1 lb snow peas

ASSEMBLY

2 Tbsp cold butter, cubed

Carnitas Lonja
Alejandro Paredes

CARNITAS LONJA has a long list of accolades, including a spot on *Esquire* magazine's list of best new restaurants in 2017, yet it remains unspoiled by the attention and widely regarded as a "secret" destination for avid foodies. All thanks to chef-owner Alejandro Paredes, who got the nod as a James Beard semifinalist for Best Chef Texas in 2020. After one visit, you'll quickly discover why this restaurant is lauded.

Order at the walk-up window or take a seat at one of the outdoor picnic tables or indoor four tops and prepare for a culinary trip to Mexico. A study in precision comes to the table: slow-cooked pork, house-made corn tortillas, perfectly poached octopus and shrimp tostadas, simply seasoned guacamole, and two or three refreshing aguas frescas. Paredes and his crew (mainly family) create big flavors from minimal ingredients, as has been the case for generations. As a kid, he enjoyed helping out in the kitchen when they were still living in Morelia, Mexico, yet he made a practical decision to earn a business degree in his second home in San Antonio. In just a few years, he rethought his journey and decided to relearn culinary basics at several San Antonio fine-dining kitchens, with the plan to open his own dining spot. While *lonja* translates to "love handle," Paredes leaves it vague as to whether it's a reference to the cut of meat or the result of eating it. And who cares? When food this good hits your lips, the only utterable word is the universal "mmm."

Camaroncillas SERVES 6–8

Instead of calling these *quesadillas de camarones* (shrimp quesadillas) as they do in many U.S. restaurants, Paredes encourages his guests to call the dish *camaroncillas*, the name used in the coastal area of Guerrero, Mexico, where it originated. "Not a lot of people combine seafood and cheese," he explains. "The name is a combination of the Spanish word for shrimp (camarones) with the word quesadilla."

FILLING Heat 2 tablespoons oil in a small skillet over medium-high heat. Add onions and sauté for 3 minutes. Transfer to a bowl.

Heat remaining 1 tablespoon oil in the skillet over medium-high heat. Add shrimp and sauté for 3–4 minutes, until opaque and cooked through. Transfer to a cutting board and chop. Add to the bowl of onions.

Heat the same skillet over medium heat. Add chorizo and sauté for 3–5 minutes, until fully cooked. Drain, then add to the bowl of onions and shrimp. Allow to cool, then mix in the cheese and set aside.

CORN TORTILLAS In a large bowl, combine tortilla mix, salt, and 1 cup water and mix for 2 minutes to form a soft dough. (If the dough is dry or crumbly, add 1 tablespoon of water at a time until it is soft.)

Place the dough on a work surface. Divide the dough into 6–8 uniform balls, then place balls back in the bowl and cover with a damp towel as you work.

Place a dough ball on a tortilla press and press it into a ⅛-inch-thick disk. (Alternatively, place a dough ball between 2 plates covered with plastic wrap or use a rolling pin to roll out the dough.) Repeat with remaining dough balls.

ASSEMBLY Place 2 tablespoons filling in the center of a tortilla, leaving a ¼-inch border to seal the edges. Fold the tortilla over to make a half-moon shape and pinch the edges to seal securely. Repeat with remaining tortillas and filling.

Heat oil in a deep fryer to a temperature of 350°F.

Working in batches to avoid overcrowding and averting your face from the hot oil, gently lower camaroncillas into oil and deep-fry for 5 minutes. (Alternatively, heat 2 inches of oil in a skillet. Add camaroncillas and fry for 3½ minutes on each side, until golden brown.) Transfer to a paper towel-lined plate to drain. Set aside until cool to the touch.

Slit each camaroncilla lengthwise and garnish with cabbage and cilantro.

FILLING

3 Tbsp canola oil (divided)
¼ onion, thinly sliced
½ lb medium-sized shrimp, peeled and deveined
¼ lb chorizo, chopped
¼ cup shredded Oaxaca cheese

CORN TORTILLAS

2 cups dry corn tortilla mix (preferably Maseca)
¼ tsp table salt

ASSEMBLY

Filling (see here)
Corn Tortillas (see here)
1½–2 cups canola oil, for frying
1 cup finely shredded green cabbage, for garnish
½ cup chopped cilantro, for garnish

Michoacán-Style Carnitas (Carnitas Estilo Michoacán) SERVES 4

CARNITAS Heat a large Dutch oven over high heat. Add pork and sear for 7–10 minutes on each side to form an even crust. Add lard and allow it to melt completely. Pour in 2 cups water, add salt, and bring to a boil. Cover and boil for 2 hours, reducing the heat, if necessary, to prevent the mixture from boiling over.

Reduce to low heat and simmer for 1 hour. Remove the pot from the heat and set aside for 2 hours to rest.

PICKLED RED ONIONS In a medium glass bowl, combine vinegar and sugar and stir until dissolved. Stir in salt, oregano, and onions. Set aside to marinate at room temperature for 20–30 minutes. Leftover onions can be stored in a covered container in the refrigerator for up to 3 days.

ASSEMBLY Discard liquid from meat. Transfer meat to a cutting board and shred.

Heat tortillas in a hot skillet. When heated, place each tortilla on a separate plate. Divide meat evenly between tortillas. Top each with pickled red onions and a squeeze of lime. Finish with your favorite red or green salsa.

CARNITAS
2 lbs pork butt, ideally 1–2 large chunks
1 lb seasoned or unseasoned lard
¼ cup table salt

PICKLED RED ONIONS
1 cup white vinegar
Pinch of sugar
Pinch of salt
Pinch of dried Mexican oregano
1 red onion, thinly sliced

ASSEMBLY
Carnitas (see here)
8 Corn Tortillas (see page 112)
Pickled Red Onions (see here)
2 limes, quartered
Salsa

Clementine

John Russ and Elise Russ

CLEMENTINE FULLY embodies the descriptors *seasonal menu*, *a neighborhood vibe*, *global flavors*, and *family owned and operated*. Hidden in a cluster of shops on a busy, tree-lined road, it's easy to pass by. Once you've experienced it, though, you'll notice Clementine on every drive by and wish you were back at a table.

Chefs John and Elise Russ have formal culinary degrees, share an appetite for food and the outdoors, and met in a professional resort kitchen. These days, their passions include raising their three young children, serving the community as volunteers and mentors, and preparing Southern menus from their well-planned kitchen at Clementine. Here, we see John's New Orleans roots through heritage-driven recipes with modern twists (such as hush puppies served with sumac-herb *labneh* and turnips topped with sesame seed streusel) and an array of vegetarian dishes (often tested at home for Elise and later incorporated into the restaurant menu). The popular Feed Me option is a full-on global feast that might include the smoked bacon flame tart,

red lentil chaat, marker swordfish with black aioli, and vanilla crème brûlée with *kataifi* (a Greek honey and nut pastry) on the side. It's course after course of chefs' selections served family-style at a steady pace to the table until you collectively cry uncle.

Desserts such as cardamom donuts with candied limequats and coffee ice cream are Elise's lifelong celebration of texture and temperature contrasts, and the fun of ending a meal with a sweet smile. The result is a farm-fresh, locally driven, and tightly honed menu.

White Mushroom Salad SERVES 3–4

A great party pleaser as well as a simple salad for last-minute guests, this was the Russes' go-to salad when entertaining. They put it on their very first menu at Clementine, never realizing it would become one of their signature dishes.

Remove mushroom stems and reserve. Very thinly slice mushroom caps, then thinly slice stems. Place caps and stems in a large serving bowl. Add parsley, onions, and radishes.

Using a sharp knife, carefully remove the top and bottom of pomegranate. Serrate the skin, then tear the segments apart. Over a bowl of cold water, pop the seeds into the bowl. Remove any skin or pith that falls into the bowl. Drain, then pat seeds dry with a paper towel. Add 1 cup seeds to the bowl containing the veggies. The undressed salad can be covered and stored in the refrigerator until you're ready to serve.

In a separate bowl, combine oil, lemon juice, salt, and pepper and mix well. Add dressing to salad and toss gently. Finish with pecorino (or Parmesan).

8 oz button mushrooms

Bunch of Italian parsley, leaves only and finely chopped

½ red onion, thinly sliced

2 small red radishes, trimmed and very thinly sliced

1 pomegranate

½ cup extra-virgin olive oil

Juice of 2 lemons (preferably Meyer lemons), strained (about ½ cup)

Kosher salt and black pepper, to taste

3 oz pecorino or Parmesan, finely shaven

Cavatelli with Broccoli Top Pesto
and Sichuan Peppercorns, p. 78–79

Cavatelli with Broccoli Top Pesto and Sichuan Peppercorns SERVES 6–8

This recipe requires a gnocchi board, which you can buy for about $5. (You won't regret having it in your arsenal of essential kitchen tools.) If you don't have one, the dough can be rolled on a flat board and indented with the tines of a fork.

CAVATELLI
2 cups ricotta
2 egg yolks
1 egg
4 cups "00" flour, plus extra for dusting (all-purpose flour will do just fine)
Pinch of sea salt

BROCCOLI TOP PESTO
1 lb broccoli heads with stems
½ cup finely grated Parmesan
1 Tbsp ground Aleppo pepper
¼–½ cup extra-virgin olive oil
1 Tbsp aged balsamic vinegar
Sea salt and black pepper, to taste

CAVATELLI In a stand mixer fitted with the hook attachment, combine ricotta, egg yolks, and egg and mix for 2 minutes. Add flour and salt and mix for another 12 minutes at medium speed, until dense and tacky.

Transfer the dough to a stainless-steel bowl and cover with plastic wrap. Set aside to rest at room temperature for at least 20 minutes.

On a lightly floured work surface, divide the dough into 10 equal balls. Cover unused balls with plastic wrap or a damp cloth. Roll out a dough ball into a long log, ½ inch in diameter. Repeat with remaining balls, then line them up in rows.

With a long, sharp knife, cut the logs into ¾-inch segments. Roll each dumpling between your palms, creating uniform balls.

Dust the gnocchi board with flour and hold it firmly by the handle. Using the thumb on your dominant hand, roll the dumplings down the gnocchi board and push firmly in the center so that the dough elongates with grooves. (This motion will also cause the dough to roll over your thumb, creating a small indentation or tunnel in the center—this makes a great vessel for the sauce.) Repeat this process until all the balls are rolled and shaped.

Bring a large saucepan of salted water to a rapid boil. Add cavatelli and cook for 3–4 minutes, until they float to the surface. Using a slotted spoon, transfer to a baking sheet lined with parchment paper. If not using immediately, toss cavatelli with a drizzle of oil and refrigerate in a sealed container for up to 4 days.

BROCCOLI TOP PESTO Using a very sharp knife, carefully shave off broccoli tops and reserve about 1 cup. Unused broccoli stems can be used in another dish.

In a bowl, combine broccoli tops, Parmesan, Aleppo pepper, oil, and vinegar. Season with salt and black pepper. Set aside to rest at room temperature for at least 30 minutes, until oil has emulsified. Pesto can be covered and stored in the refrigerator for up to 5 days.

ASSEMBLY Preheat oven to 350°F.

Spread out pecans on a baking sheet and toast for 8 minutes, until golden brown and nutty.

Heat oil and 2 tablespoons butter in a skillet over medium-high heat, until butter begins to bubble. Add cavatelli and lightly toast for 3–5 minutes, untouched. Gently toss cavatelli and sauté for another 3 minutes, until light golden brown.

Reduce heat to medium-low. Add garlic and shallots and sauté for 30 seconds, until fragrant. Add ¼ cup stock (or water) and simmer for 1–2 minutes, until slightly reduced and thickened to a saucy consistency. If too thick, add more stock. Stir in parsley, then season with salt and black pepper. Add remaining 2 tablespoons butter, gently swirl butter in the skillet to mix, and remove from heat.

Place the cooked pasta mixture in a large serving bowl. Lightly sprinkle pepper flakes and pecans over top. Shave Parmesan over pasta and finish with as much pesto as you like.

Serve immediately with extra pepper flakes, pecans, grated Parmesan, and remaining pesto on the table.

ASSEMBLY

½ cup pecan halves, plus extra to serve

¼ cup extra-virgin olive oil

¼ cup (½ stick) butter (divided)

2 cups Cavatelli (see here)

1 clove garlic, minced

1 small shallot, finely chopped

¼–½ cup chicken stock or water

Bunch of Italian parsley, leaves only

Salt and black pepper, to taste

1–2 tsp Sichuan pepper flakes, plus extra to serve

4 oz Parmesan, plus extra to serve

Broccoli Top Pesto (see here)

Davila's BBQ

Edward Davila and Adrian Davila

DAVILA'S BBQ waves its vaquero flag, linking its cooking style to the Texas-Mexican cowboys who practiced the original snout-to-tail cookery. In the 1970s, Edward Davila took over the Davila's BBQ business his father, Raul, had begun twenty years earlier. Today, Edward's son Adrian is now by his side, breathing new life into the family business with zeal for his ancestors and their traditions.

Like the two generations before him, Adrian ensures that their classic family sausage recipes are unscathed by modernity (to retain their outer pop and inner juiciness), that the old smokers keep chugging on cords of wood (and not gas), and that regulars feel at home and newcomers feel welcome. He has also made several television appearances, including a win on Food Network's *BBQ Blitz*, and authored the cookbook *Cowboy Barbecue: Fire & Smoke from the Original Texas Vaqueros*. With every activity, Adrian remains focused on raising the profile of his family smokehouse and their vaquero way of cooking.

What makes the cooking style so traditional? For one, the spice blend in the house BBQ sauce includes cumin—a Moorish influence from old Spain—and Mediterranean oregano. Then, there's the smoked lamb ribs, a connection to the lamb and goat in interior Mexican cuisine. Or consider the dry rub made with cayenne pepper, an ingredient first cultivated in Mexico seven thousand years ago. Together, these elements make up the BBQ tradition and the Davila family honor that embodies the vaquero ways.

Davila's Original BBQ Sauce MAKES ABOUT 2 CUPS

Davila's BBQ has been serving up this original recipe since Raul Davila opened the doors in 1959. Slather it on chicken, pork, beef, lamb, or even salmon. It's *that* good.

1½ tsp margarine
½ cup tomato paste
½ cup ketchup
½ cup tomato juice
2 Tbsp Worcestershire sauce
¼ cup sugar
¼ cup cornstarch
2 Tbsp dill pickle juice
1 Tbsp prepared yellow mustard
¾ tsp black pepper
¾ tsp garlic powder
¾ tsp ground cumin
½ tsp dried oregano
½ tsp kosher salt

Melt margarine in a large saucepan over medium-low heat. Stir in tomato paste, ketchup, tomato juice, Worcestershire, and ½ cup water.

In a large bowl, combine remaining ingredients. Mix until sugar and salt are dissolved. Stir into the tomato mixture. Cook over low heat for 10 minutes, until sauce thickens.

Serve immediately. Any leftover sauce can be stored in an airtight container in the refrigerator for up to 10 days.

Dry-Rubbed Smoked Pork Ribs SERVES 4–6

The key to this recipe is to cook the ribs long enough for the meat to fall off the bone, but not so long that they dry out. The smoke will do the talking in the finished rack.

DAVILA'S SIGNATURE BBQ RUB Combine all ingredients in a bowl and mix well. The rub can be stored in an airtight container for up to a year.

SMOKED PORK RIBS Rub the entire surface of ribs with dry rub. Wrap in plastic wrap and refrigerate for 12–24 hours.

    Preheat smoker to 275°F using your favorite wood.

    Smoke ribs, meat side down, for 1½ hours. Flip over and cook for another 1½ hours to an internal temperature of 195°F. If meat appears to be drying out, wrap ribs in aluminum foil for the final quarter of the smoking time. Check for doneness by picking ribs up from the center of the slab. When properly done, the slab should fold over. If it bends slightly, it needs more time.

DAVILA'S SIGNATURE BBQ RUB
1½ cups table salt
⅓ cup black pepper
3 Tbsp cayenne pepper

SMOKED PORK RIBS
1 (3–3½-lb) slab pork spare ribs, silver skin removed
¼ cup Davila's Signature BBQ Rub (see here)

The Esquire Tavern

Chris Hill and Stephan Mendez

CLOSED FOR only five of its nearly ninety-year history, The Esquire Tavern echoes with the spirit of old San Antonio. You can easily imagine former patrons sitting at the one-hundred-foot bar, the longest in Texas, chatting with a bartender as he slides a Pearl or Lone Star their way. First opened in 1933, the day Prohibition ended, The Esquire was opulent yet egalitarian, with its pressed copper ceilings, elaborately carved woodwork, flocked velvet wallpaper, narrow booths, and terracotta floor tiles. It remained that way, nearly untouched and poorly maintained, into the 2000s.

In 2011, after several years of renovation, its new owner, Chris Hill, reopened the restored tavern, returning it to its glory days and beyond with significant upgrades to the Riverwalk patio, bar, lighting, and menu. Today, The Esquire Tavern's signature mixologists serve booze that's a bit more bougie and drafts that are craft.

Plus, there's an elevated bar food menu. The snacks have evolved to include shrimp cocktail, tenderloin steak, and a burger topped with a fried egg. But the drinks and nonjudgmental vibe still entice eclectic crowds who will happily while away slow hours at the long bar, on the patio, or even in a cozy booth. Others simply pop in for a quick, restorative quaff. Some things never change. And that's the beauty of this historic spot.

THE ESQUIRE TAVERN Chester Copperpot, p. 86 and Fancy C.V.S. (Cherry Vodka Sour), p. 87

Chester Copperpot SERVES 1

¾ oz cognac
¾ oz Jamaican pot still gold rum
½ oz white overproof rum
¾ oz coconut syrup
½ oz The Bitter Truth Golden
    Falernum liqueur
½ oz orange juice
¼ oz lemon juice
½ oz Pedro Ximénez sherry
Sprig of mint, for garnish
Thin orange slice, for garnish

Pour cognac, gold rum, white rum, syrup, Falernum, orange juice, and lemon juice into a cocktail shaker. Shake vigorously for 5 seconds and pour into a hurricane glass, then fill glass with crushed ice. Gently pour sherry over the back of a spoon onto the surface of the cocktail. Garnish with mint and orange slice.

Fancy C.V.S. (Cherry Vodka Sour) SERVES 1

Pour all ingredients except flower and cherry into a cocktail shaker.
Shake vigorously for 5 seconds. Serve over ice in a rocks glass.
Garnish with flower and cherry (if using).

1½ oz vodka
¾ oz lemon juice
½ oz sour cherry wine
½ oz Palo Cortado sherry
½ oz simple syrup
1 tsp maraschino liqueur
Orchid flower, for garnish (optional)
Cherry, for garnish (optional)

The Friendly Spot
Ice House

Jody Bailey Newman and Steve Newman

THIS OUTDOOR venue in the heart of hip South-town is truly the sum of its many parts: craft beer heaven, cocktail bar, kids' playground, big-screen sports center, and pup-welcoming lounge. Indeed, it's friendly and the spot to be on lazy afternoons and chill-out evenings. With two hundred brews to choose from, seventy-six of them on tap, the menu offers plenty for even the most discerning beer lovers. Cocktails and Friendly Frozens are also on tap, and the wine selection has an outpouring of supporters.

The kitchen, open until midnight, serves burgers, nachos, and other snacks you might expect from a bar menu. They even offer veggie-, kid-, and pet-friendly fare. Owners Jody and Steve Newman exude the sociability in the name, as do their loyal staff members, who keep the atmosphere light and open to all. Jody has become a bar industry spokesperson, serving on city and state task forces and

advocating for bar owners. Her ongoing leadership of citywide Break Fast & Launch, the nation's first culinary business accelerator, offers industry newbies the pro bono expertise of hospitality insiders who review their business plans.

"But what exactly is an *ice house*?" you may ask. Well, it's an old Texas term for a gathering place where neighbors can be friends and friends can be themselves. The Friendly Spot Ice House defines it perfectly.

Mahi Mahi Tacos SERVES 2

The firm texture of mahi mahi holds up well to hands-on eating, but halibut, swordfish, and tuna also work well. Just avoid delicate, flaky fish that will get lost in the sauce. And napkins are a must.

SLAW
½ small head green cabbage, thinly sliced
½ small head red cabbage, thinly sliced
½ large carrot, shaved into ribbons
1 cup + 1 Tbsp apple cider vinegar (divided)
1 Tbsp Kosher salt, plus extra to taste
1 Tbsp black pepper, plus extra to taste

PICO DE GALLO
5 Roma tomatoes, chopped
5 cloves garlic, minced
3 serrano peppers, finely chopped
1 small red onion, chopped
Bunch of cilantro, finely chopped
2 Tbsp kosher salt, plus extra to taste
2 Tbsp black pepper, plus extra to taste
Juice of 3 limes

CILANTRO-LIME SAUCE
Juice of 3 limes
¼ cup apple cider vinegar
½ small yellow onion
12 cloves garlic, peeled
2 serrano peppers
Bunch of cilantro
Kosher salt and black pepper, to taste

SLAW In a large bowl, combine green cabbage, red cabbage, carrots, 1 cup vinegar, and 1 tablespoon each of salt and pepper. Taste before serving and season with an additional 1 tablespoon vinegar and more salt and pepper if needed.

PICO DE GALLO Combine all ingredients in a large bowl and mix well. Set aside to rest for at least 5 minutes. Season with more salt and pepper if needed.

CILANTRO-LIME SAUCE Combine lime juice, vinegar, and ¼ cup ice-cold water in a blender. Add onion, garlic, peppers, and cilantro and blend until smooth. Season with salt and black pepper.

FRIED MAHI MAHI Combine spices in a large bowl. Add fish and toss to coat.

Heat oil in a skillet over medium-high heat. Add fish and cook for 3 minutes on each side, until golden and the internal temperature is 145°F. Transfer to a rack to drain.

ASSEMBLY Heat a tortilla on a griddle or in a cast-iron skillet over medium-high heat until soft. Wrap in a dish towel to keep warm. Repeat with remaining tortillas.

Place 2 tortillas on each serving plate. Spoon slaw in the center of each, top with a piece of fish, a spoonful of pico de gallo, and a sprinkle of queso fresco. Drizzle sauce on top.

Serve immediately.

FRIED MAHI MAHI
¼ cup ground cumin
¼ cup onion powder
¼ cup paprika
2 Tbsp kosher salt
2 Tbsp cayenne pepper
2 Tbsp garlic powder
4 (4-oz) mahi mahi fillets, cut into thick strips
¼ cup neutral frying oil

ASSEMBLY
4 large corn tortillas
1–2 cups Slaw (see here)
Fried Mahi Mahi (see here)
¼ cup Pico de Gallo (see here)
¼ cup queso fresco
Cilantro-Lime Sauce (see here)

Blood Orange Mule SERVES 1

When you're seeking to create a night-out vibe from the comforts of home, look no further than this original take on a traditional Moscow Mule.

BLOOD ORANGE SYRUP Combine purée and sugar in a saucepan. Simmer over medium heat for 10–20 minutes, stirring occasionally, until reduced to 1 cup. Set aside to cool. Leftover syrup can be stored in a covered jar in the refrigerator for up to 1 week.

BLOOD ORANGE MULE Add vodka, juice, and syrup to a tall glass. Fill with ice. Top with ginger beer. Sip responsibly.

BLOOD ORANGE SYRUP
1½ cups canned or frozen blood orange purée, strained
½ cup sugar

BLOOD ORANGE MULE
1½ oz your favorite vodka (we like Derel)
2 oz lime juice
½ oz Blood Orange Syrup (see here)
Ginger beer

Full Belly

James Moore (R)
and Blade Haddock (L)

CHEF JAMES MOORE and restaurateur Blade
Haddock combined each of their thirty-plus years
of culinary experience and passion for hospitality
into a creative new endeavor. Despite opening their
first joint venture weeks before the COVID lockdown,
Full Belly returned to service seven months later
with the high intensity of a new restaurant and the
polish of a timeless classic.

The unassuming setting in a retail center belies
the uniquely artistic interior and confident scratch
kitchen. Bright, local artwork and murals deck
the walls with vibrant visual dimension, a nod to
Moore and Haddock's appreciation for creativity.
There's culinary art on the plates, whether it's the
house-baked pastries, slow braises, or focaccias
from the wood-fired oven. The all-day breakfast
menu includes everything from rousing house-
ground maple fennel sausage to pecan pie French
toast. Bracing midday meals of plump mussels
and fries, fried trout, hearty burgers, and a savory
bread pudding with roasted chicken, leeks, and
portobellos round things out.

If you're looking for inspired drinks, the cocktail
menu brims with luscious options. There's a flashy
side of inventive cocktails such as the white rum-
based Mr. Boombastic (call it fantastic), lip-pucker-
ing Say Anything, and gin-viting Last Tango in Paris
(all clearly named for cultural reference buffs).
The Full Belly experience is an accessible culinary
entryway to fine-dining food with none of the fuss
and all of the finesse.

FULL BELLY Baked Eggs in Roasted Garlic Cream with Pepper Relish, p. 96

Baked Eggs in Roasted Garlic Cream with Pepper Relish SERVES 4

This rich take on the classic French *oeufs en cocotte* is sure to become your go-to brunch dish for special guests and occasions.

ROASTED GARLIC

2 large heads garlic

Olive oil, for drizzling

Kosher salt (preferably Diamond Crystal)

Black pepper

ROASTED GARLIC CREAM

½ cup (1 stick) salted butter

½ cup all-purpose flour

2 qts heavy cream

Roasted Garlic (see here)

2 Tbsp dried thyme

1 Tbsp kosher salt (preferably Diamond Crystal)

RED HOT SAUCE

5 cloves garlic, peeled

4 Roma tomatoes, quartered

2 red jalapeño peppers, quartered

1 small yellow onion, cut into eighths

Extra-virgin olive oil, for coating

1 Tbsp red wine vinegar

1 Tbsp kosher salt, plus extra if needed

1 Tbsp black pepper

Juice of 1 lime, plus extra if needed

ROASTED GARLIC Preheat oven to 350°F.

Cut and discard the top of the garlic heads to expose the top of the cloves. Place on a sheet of aluminum foil and drizzle oil over each head. Lightly season with salt and pepper, then wrap tightly in the foil to seal. Roast for 30–45 minutes, until cloves are soft when gently squeezed. Set aside to cool, then unwrap and squeeze each head to release cloves. Set aside.

ROASTED GARLIC CREAM Melt butter in a saucepan over low heat. Add flour and whisk continuously until the mixture has the consistency of wet sand. (The mixture is called a *roux*.) Set aside.

In a heavy-bottomed saucepan, combine remaining ingredients and simmer gently over medium-low heat for 30 minutes.

Whisk in roux and simmer for another 5 minutes to thicken. Strain sauce through a fine-mesh sieve and set aside.

RED HOT SAUCE Preheat oven to 375°F.

In a large bowl, combine garlic, tomatoes, jalapeños, and onions. Add enough oil to lightly coat and mix well. Transfer mixture to a baking sheet and spread out in a single layer. Roast for 15 minutes, until lightly golden. Set aside to cool.

Transfer to a blender, add remaining ingredients, and purée until smooth. Season with more salt or lime juice, if needed, to achieve a balanced flavor.

PEPPER RELISH Preheat oven to 375°F.

Rub peppers with 2 tablespoons oil and place them on a baking sheet. Sprinkle with salt and pepper. Roast 20 to 30 minutes until blistered and lightly charred. Immediately place peppers in a zipper bag to steam until cool to the touch.

Once cooled, gently remove and discard skins, then pull stems and remove seeds. Resist the urge to rinse the peppers as that will dilute the flavor.

Cut cleaned peppers into 1-inch long by ¼-inch wide strips. Place into a medium mixing bowl. Add remaining ingredients and mix well, then season with salt and pepper to taste.

ASSEMBLY Preheat oven to 450°F. Set out 4 (7-inch) au gratin dishes or other baking dishes on a baking sheet.

Evenly distribute ham (or lardons) and shallots into each dish. Top each with 1 cup roasted garlic cream, then swirl the dishes to spread out the mixture evenly. Carefully crack 3 eggs into each dish, taking care not to break yolks. Give the dish a gentle shimmy to cover the egg whites in the sauce (yolks will remain visible). Bake for 7 minutes, until whites are set while yolks remain loose. If needed, bake for another 2 minutes.

Garnish each dish with ⅓ cup Parmesan, drizzle hot sauce on top, sprinkle with parsley (or chives), and finish with pepper relish.

Serve with toast. (And be sure to break the yolks and swipe the toast through the mixture for the ultimate bite.)

PEPPER RELISH

2 red bell peppers

2 yellow bell peppers

1 cup + 2 Tbsp olive oil

Kosher salt and black pepper

1 Tbsp parsley, chopped

1 Tbsp chives, chopped

1 Tbsp fresh oregano leaves, chopped

2 shallots, peeled and finely chopped

⅓ cup red wine vinegar

ASSEMBLY

1 cup diced ham or cooked lardons

2–3 shallots, chopped (½ cup)

4 cups Roasted Garlic Cream
   (see here)

12 eggs

1⅓ cups shredded Parmesan

½ cup Red Hot Sauce (see here)

Bunch of Italian parsley, chopped,
   or ½ cup chopped chives

Pepper Relish (see here)

8 slices sourdough or any thick
   crusty bread, toasted and buttered,
   cut diagonally

12-Hour Brisket on White Cheddar Grits with Chimichurri SERVES 4–6

Brisket is king in Texas, most commonly prepared as smoked barbecue, yet this recipe closely resembles a Sunday pot roast. It's accompanied with good ol' Southern grits and a bright and punchy Argentine chimichurri-herb hybrid sauce. Plan ahead for this recipe, knowing full well that good things come to those who wait.

BRISKET

½ cup kosher salt (preferably Diamond Crystal)

½ cup black pepper

3 Tbsp garlic powder

3 Tbsp onion powder

1 (4-lb) beef brisket, untrimmed

4 large carrots, quartered

3 yellow onions, quartered

1 whole head celery, cut crosswise into five chunks

10 sprigs thyme or 2 Tbsp dried

10 sprigs oregano or 2 Tbsp dried

10 juniper berries

6 bay leaves

4 star anise

3 cups dry red wine (preferably Cabernet)

1 cup balsamic vinegar

¼ cup tomato paste

WHITE CHEDDAR GRITS

5 cups whole milk

5 cups chicken stock

2 cups stone-ground white grits

4 cups shredded sharp white cheddar

3 Tbsp kosher salt

BRISKET In a small bowl, combine salt, pepper, garlic powder, and onion powder. Rub mixture over brisket. Wrap in plastic wrap and refrigerate for at least 4 hours or overnight.

Preheat oven to 250°F.

Unwrap brisket from plastic and place in a large ovenproof Dutch oven. (The pan must be tall enough so the liquids just cover the brisket.) Add remaining ingredients and enough water to just cover meat, then bring to a boil. Immediately remove from heat and cover with a tight-fitting lid. Ensure a tight seal with aluminum foil if necessary. Place on the middle rack of the oven and cook for at least 12 hours, until fork tender.

Using two large, sturdy, slotted instruments, such as spatulas or spoons, carefully transfer brisket in one piece to a baking sheet. Set aside to rest and cool, uncovered, for at least 1 hour.

Meanwhile, strain braising liquid into another pot and discard solids. Set aside liquid to cool for 30 minutes, then use a ladle to skim off and discard the fat from the surface. Simmer the liquid over medium heat for 30 minutes and continue to skim off fat from the surface, until thickened and reduced by two-thirds. (This is known as a *demi-glace*.) Remove from heat.

WHITE CHEDDAR GRITS In a heavy-bottomed saucepan, bring milk and stock to a boil over medium-high heat. Reduce to a simmer and slowly add grits, whisking continuously. Reduce to low heat and simmer for 30 minutes, stirring frequently, until grits have softened and the consistency is still a bit loose.

Remove from heat and stir in cheese and salt. Cover the pan with a towel or aluminum foil to keep warm.

CHIMICHURRI Combine all ingredients in a blender and add ¼ cup water. Purée until smooth.

ASSEMBLY Cut brisket lengthwise into wide strips, trimming away the biggest layers of fat. (It's okay to leave some for flavor.) Cut the strips crosswise into large cubes. Add brisket to the pot of demi-glace.

Return the pot to a simmer, turning brisket several times to coat. Add butter and stir, until emulsified into a velvety sauce. (Note: This sauce will hold for about 5 minutes off the heat until ready to serve. If you plan to serve the dish later, bring the liquid back to a simmer and add butter just before serving.)

Place a bed of grits at the center of each serving plate. Place about 10 ounces of brisket on top of grits, slightly off-center. Spoon several tablespoons demi-glace over brisket, then spoon 1–2 tablespoons chimichurri on top of brisket. Garnish with cilantro.

CHIMICHURRI
Bunch of cilantro, trimmed and
  roughly chopped
Bunch of Italian parsley, trimmed and
  roughly chopped
5 large cloves garlic, peeled
1 Tbsp chili flakes
1 Tbsp kosher salt
  (preferably Diamond Crystal)
¼ cup extra-virgin olive oil
¼ cup red wine vinegar

ASSEMBLY
½ cup (1 stick) salted butter, cubed
Cilantro, for garnish

Gunslingers
Stephen Paprocki

CHEF STEPHEN PAPROCKI is a busy guy. The seasoned chef worked his way up through top hotel restaurants, headed corporate kitchens, and now helms Gunslingers. His Texas Black Gold Garlic is one of only fourteen black garlic producers in the nation, now offering fifteen products from Texas-grown garlic. Through a heat- and humidity-controlled process, whole heads of garlic are transformed into fermented, caramelized, and flavorful umami bombs. (In fact, the black garlic is sprinkled generously throughout the Gunslingers menu.)

But that's not all. As president of Chef Cooperatives, Paprocki leads a group of like-minded chefs who host charitable dinners to support local farmers and producers. And he has been named a voluntary Chef Ambassador for the World Heritage Office, representing San Antonio's status as a UNESCO City of Gastronomy on the international stage. If you're counting, that's the equivalent of four full-time jobs.

At Gunslingers, diners get a sense of Paprocki's ambition through a broad menu of casual dining hits. This includes eleven types of seasoned wings, three kinds of mac 'n' cheese, seven chicken sandwiches, and as many burgers. Plus requisite sides, salads, and desserts. And best of all, the meal can be enjoyed in Gunslingers's garden oasis, one of San Antonio's prettiest alcoves.

Black Garlic Coffee-Blackened Wings SERVES 2

These versatile wings can be cooked using a deep fryer, an oven, or an air fryer. For instructions on cooking in the latter two ways, see the tip boxes below.

COFFEE-BLACKENING SPICE In a bowl, combine all ingredients thoroughly. Makes 1 cup. Store any leftover spice blend in an airtight container for up to 6 months.

COFFEE-BLACKENED WINGS Heat oil in a deep fryer or deep saucepan to a temperature of 350°F.

Wash and pat dry wings. Averting your face from the hot oil, gently lower wings into oil and deep-fry for 8 minutes, until golden brown and crispy with an internal temperature of 165°F. Using a slotted spoon, transfer wings to a large bowl and toss gently with seasoning to coat entirely.

Transfer to a serving platter and serve immediately with carrot and celery sticks and blue cheese dressing.

COFFEE-BLACKENING SPICE

¾ cup ground coffee

2 Tbsp cayenne pepper

2 Tbsp onion powder

2 Tbsp Texas Black Gold Garlic Black Garlic Powder

2 Tbsp dried thyme

2 Tbsp dried basil

2 Tbsp paprika

COFFEE-BLACKENED WINGS

Corn, peanut, or safflower oil, for deep-frying

8 chicken wings, cut into drumsticks and wingettes

½ cup Coffee-Blackening Spice (see here)

Carrot and celery sticks, to serve

Blue cheese dressing, to serve

OVEN BAKE Preheat oven to 400°F. Line a baking sheet with aluminum foil and place a metal rack over the foil. Coat the rack with cooking spray. Place wings in a large bowl and toss with 1 tablespoon vegetable oil. Arrange wings in a single layer on the rack. Bake 45 minutes, until golden brown and crispy with an internal temperature of 165°F. Follow remaining instructions in the method above.

AIR FRY Preheat air fryer to 400°F for 2 minutes. Place wings in a large bowl, drizzle with 1 tablespoon vegetable oil, and toss to coat. Add wings to fryer in a single layer and cook for 10 minutes. Carefully open the fryer and flip the wings over. Cook for another 8 minutes, until golden brown and crispy with an internal temperature of 165°F. Follow remaining instructions in the method above.

Black Garlic Brownies SERVES 8

The combination may sound strange, but the flavor is anything but. Black garlic adds moisture to the batter and imparts a sweet, earthy flavor reminiscent of fine balsamic vinegar syrup. Give this a try, and you're certain to become a fan.

Preheat oven to 325°F. Lightly grease 8 ramekins or small ovenproof dishes with cooking spray.

In a medium bowl, combine flour, cocoa powder, sugar, confectioners' sugar, garlic powder, and salt.

In a large bowl, whisk eggs, oil, vanilla, and 2 tablespoons water. Sprinkle the dry mixture over the wet mixture and stir until just combined.

Pour batter evenly into the ramekins and, using a spatula, smooth the tops. Set ramekins in a roasting pan filled halfway with water and bake for 40–48 minutes, until a toothpick comes out with only a few crumbs attached.

Serve hot with a scoop of ice cream, chocolate sauce, and a maraschino cherry (if using) on top.

Nonstick cooking spray
¾ cup all-purpose flour
⅔ cup cocoa powder, sifted
½ cup sugar
½ cup confectioners' sugar, sifted
¼ cup Texas Black Gold Garlic Black Garlic Powder
¾ tsp sea salt
2 eggs
½ cup canola oil
½ tsp vanilla extract
½ gallon vanilla ice cream, to serve (optional)
Chocolate syrup or sauce, to serve (optional)
8 maraschino cherries, to serve (optional)

Jazz, TX

Doc Watkins and Jake Corney

WALK DOWNSTAIRS at the Pearl Bottling Department building, then through the curtains into this snazzy club, and you'll find yourself in another world. It's a universe where music is always performed live, cocktails are made by hand, and snacks go well beyond the basics. It is a jazz club, first and foremost, but the accoutrements synchronize into a full-blown evening out.

Owner-musician Doc Watkins built the club to celebrate all things jazz, bringing noteworthy performers from around the globe to perform Texas swing, straight-up jazz, blues, big band, and so much more. Most nights, Watkins shares the stage with his quartet or eleven-piece orchestra, opening the musical gates and dance floor for the night's visiting act. The seasonal bar menu comes courtesy of cocktail impresario Jake Corney, who serves as the creative potent potable genius and makes sure the kitchen keeps up with the demand for dishes with a Texas twang.

The dining menu isn't just a sidenote either, with hearty, large plates such as tender center-cut beef fillet, spicy Creole pasta, and cherry-glazed salmon. Smaller snacks, from hummus to mini tacos, add backbeat fill, while a short list of desserts leave a lasting impression to a sweet night of music. This unexpected oasis calls you back for another sip from the delightful well.

Jazz Burger with House Pickles SERVES 2

This two-handed burger is served at the club with truffle fries on the side.

HOUSE PICKLES In a saucepan, combine vinegar, sugar, salt, and 2 cups water. Bring to a boil, stirring to dissolve sugar and salt.

Place cucumbers, garlic, dill, and butter in a 1-quart canning jar. Add pickling liquid to the jar and set aside to cool. Cover and refrigerate for at least 1 hour (but they'll taste even better after 2 days).

JAZZ BURGER Grind brisket, tenderloin, and fat in a grinder at a medium setting. (Alternatively, use a food processor to grind the meat, but do not over-process.)

In a large bowl, combine ground meat, spices, and egg yolk. Form 2 patties.

Melt butter in a cast-iron skillet over medium-high heat. Add onions and sauté for 10 minutes, until slightly caramelized. Move onions to the side of the skillet and add bacon. Cook bacon for 3 minutes total, until crispy. Stir onions often to avoid sticking and burning. Transfer bacon to a paper towel–lined plate to drain.

Add patties to the skillet and grill for 3 minutes on one side. Flip patties and move them to a different part of the skillet to cook for another 3 minutes. Flip and move again to ensure even cooking for another 3 minutes. Repeat the flip-and-move action one last time.

Top each patty with cheeses and cook until cheeses have melted.

ASSEMBLY Assemble burgers from the bottom up starting with the bottom bun, onions, burger patty, bacon, lettuce, mayo, ketchup, and pickles. Finish with the top bun.

Serve immediately.

HOUSE PICKLES
1 cup distilled white vinegar
1½ cups sugar
¼ cup kosher salt
2 hothouse cucumbers, sliced into ⅛-inch-thick rounds
5 cloves garlic, peeled
10 sprigs dill (2 oz)
½ cup (1 stick) butter

JAZZ BURGER
8 oz beef brisket meat, trimmed
2¾ oz beef tenderloin
5¼ oz beef brisket fat
1 Tbsp sweet paprika
½ Tbsp onion powder
½ Tbsp garlic powder
Pinch of kosher salt
Pinch of black pepper
1 egg yolk
1 Tbsp butter
1 small sweet yellow onion, sliced
2 (2-oz) thick-cut slices cherrywood-smoked bacon
1 oz smoked cheddar
1 oz muenster cheese

ASSEMBLY
2 potato burger buns, split and toasted
Jazz Burger (see here)
4 leaves green lettuce
1 Tbsp mayonnaise
1 Tbsp ketchup
House Pickles (see here)

Ensemble SERVES 1

Texas Hill Country peaches are legendarily sweet and flavorful. When the annual bounty arrives, the bar puts them to good use. By incorporating the peach flavor over time, you are creating a "journey cocktail" with flavors that change as the cocktail is consumed.

BASIL OIL Combine all ingredients in a glass jar and seal. Set aside to meld at room temperature. Leftover basil oil can be stored for up to 3 days. Add it to your favorite pastas, stews, or soups.

ENSEMBLE Add sugar cube to your favorite cold rocks glass. Saturate sugar cube with Angostura bitters and peach bitters, then top with a splash of soda water. Quickly muddle into a light paste. Add bourbon and lightly stir 2–3 times. Do not overmix. Add ice cube and lightly stir 2–3 times. Again, do not overmix.

Working quickly, place frozen peach as close to the bottom of the glass as possible so that it slowly begins to thaw within the bonded bourbon. Place basil leaf at the top of the cocktail and finish with oil. Enjoy!

BASIL OIL
1½ sprigs basil (¼ oz)
½ cup high-quality grapeseed oil
Small pinch of kosher salt
Small pinch of black pepper

ENSEMBLE
1 demerara sugar cube
   (preferably Gilway)
1–2 dashes Angostura bitters
1–2 dashes peach bitters
Splash of soda water
2 oz good-quality bonded bourbon
Large format ice cube
1 fresh peach slice, frozen
1 basil leaf
1–2 drops Basil Oil (see here)

La Fonda on Main
Victor Maldonado

LA FONDA stakes claim as the oldest Mexican restaurant in San Antonio, focusing on interior regional dishes and including requisite Tex-Mex for good measure. Initially opened in 1932 by sisters Virginia Berry and Nannie Randall, the hacienda-style restaurant with its verdant tree-canopied patio was spruced up in 1997 by Cappy Lawton and his Lawton Restaurant Group.

Chef Victor Maldonado's menu is part dinner at a hacienda in rural Mexico, part casual dining with friends. For quick and light fare, there are the flavorful campechana cocktail of shrimp, scallops, and octopus in toasted pasilla chile sauce and the baby spinach salad topped with mango, avocado, and a mango-citrus vinaigrette. Special occasions, on the other hand, demand more elaborate dishes such as the *pato en mole arándano*, a tender seared duck breast over a tangy cranberry mole—a taste of Thanksgiving in Mexico. Weekend brunch parties might start with a Spicy Maria (a bloody Mary made with tequila) and get going with a *mollete*

(an open-face sandwich loaded with black beans, chorizo, and cheese) and benchmark huevos rancheros and migas. An order of Tres Cafes, which has coffee ice cream topped with coffee liqueur and coffee bean shavings, finishes off the meal.

On their way to their tables, guests nod to familiar faces while groups of friends gather pre- and post-meal on the street-side patio. It's a welcoming social club where your appetite is your dues.

Beef Shank Barbacoa SERVES 4–6

Barbacoa is a weekend brunch staple in San Antonio, and this recipe brings the tradition to your kitchen. For a festive family dinner, pair this beef shank with Corn Tortillas, Guacamole, and Salsas (see page 112) and let everyone create their own tacos.

Preheat oven to 350°F.

Season shank with salt and pepper. Heat oil in an ovenproof Dutch oven over medium-high heat until oil begins to simmer. Add shank and sear on all sides until golden brown. Transfer shank to a plate and set aside.

To the same Dutch oven over medium-high heat, add garlic and sauté for 1 minute, until lightly browned. Add onions, carrots, and celery and sauté for 5 minutes until onions are translucent. Add tomatoes and cook for another 5 minutes, until tomatoes have released their juices and begun to brown. Stir in ancho chiles and pasilla chiles.

Add shank back to the pan and pour in beer. Cover and roast in the oven for 3 hours, until the internal meat temperature is 150°F. Remove from oven and set aside to rest for at least 15 minutes.

Transfer shank to a serving platter and tent with aluminum foil.

Pour braising liquid and vegetables into a blender and blend until smooth. (Alternatively, use an immersion blender). Ladle sauce over shank and serve with extra sauce on the side.

NOTE >> Ask your butcher to provide you with the whole hind shank, with the femur bone and muscle completely intact, for this memorable and authentic barbacoa dish. However, you could also use a beef shank crosscut into thick portions.

5 lbs beef hind shank (see Note)
1 Tbsp kosher salt
2 tsp black pepper
2 Tbsp vegetable oil
10 cloves garlic, peeled
1 large onion, diced into 1-inch pieces
1 carrot, diced into 1-inch pieces
3 stalks celery, diced into 1-inch pieces
3 large Roma tomatoes, diced into 1-inch pieces
2 ancho chiles, seeded and finely ground
2 pasilla chiles, seeded and finely ground
3 (12-oz) Negra Modelo beers

Corn Tortillas, Guacamole, and Salsas SERVES 4–6

These are the perfect pairings for Beef Shank Barbacoa (see page 111).

CORN TORTILLAS

1⅓ lbs fresh white corn masa
    or 2 cups dry corn tortilla mix
    (preferably Maseca)
Kosher salt, to taste

GUACAMOLE

3 Tbsp finely chopped white onions
1 serrano or jalapeño pepper,
    seeded (optional) and finely
    chopped (divided)
Kosher salt, to taste
2 large avocados, pitted and chopped
1 tsp lime juice, plus extra to taste
1 small tomato, cored, seeded,
    and finely chopped
2 Tbsp roughly chopped cilantro

ROASTED TOMATO SALSA

8 Roma tomatoes (1½ lbs)
¼ white or yellow onion
2–3 serrano peppers,
    depending on your taste
2 cloves garlic, peeled
Kosher salt, to taste

CORN TORTILLAS Preheat a comal or flat-iron griddle over medium-high heat.

If using fresh masa, place in a large bowl and knead for 2 minutes to form a soft dough. (If using dried mix, combine with salt and 1 cup water and mix for 2 minutes to form a soft dough.) If the dough is dry or crumbly, add 1 tablespoon warm water at a time until it is soft. Season with salt.

Divide the dough into 6–8 uniform balls of about 1½ inches in diameter. Place balls back in the bowl and cover with a damp towel as you work.

Place a dough ball on a tortilla press and press it into a 1/8-inch-thick disk. (Alternatively, place a dough ball between 2 plates covered with plastic wrap or use a rolling pin to roll out the dough.) Repeat with remaining dough balls.

Carefully lay a tortilla flat on the comal and cook for 30 seconds, until edges begin to firm. Using a thin spatula, flip tortilla. Cook for another minute. Transfer tortilla to a cloth-lined basket and keep covered. Repeat with remaining tortillas.

GUACAMOLE Combine onions, half the peppers, and salt in a traditional molcajete and mash to a paste. (Alternatively, use a mortar and pestle or a sturdy fork in a bowl.) Add avocados and lime juice and mash until smooth. Stir in tomatoes and cilantro. Season with more salt, lime juice, and peppers.

ROASTED TOMATO SALSA Place tomatoes, onion, peppers, and garlic on an ungreased comal or cast-iron griddle over medium-high heat. Brown vegetables for 4 minutes, turning occasionally, until vegetables have color and garlic is lightly browned. Transfer garlic to a plate. Cook vegetables for another 2–3 minutes until charred.

Transfer vegetables and garlic to a food processor or blender and pulse to a chunky consistency. Do not over-process. Season with salt.

PICO DE GALLO Mix all ingredients except salt in a bowl. Season with salt.

SALSA CRUDA Place tomatillos, 1 serrano pepper, garlic, avocado, and cilantro into a blender and process until smooth. Add lime juice, then season with salt. Add more serrano to taste.

ASSEMBLY Place beef shank on a large platter in the center of the table. Serve family-style with baskets of hot tortillas, salsas, pico de gallo, and guacamole. Let everyone pull meat from the bone and build their own tacos. *¡Delicioso!*

PICO DE GALLO

8 Roma tomatoes, finely chopped (1½ lbs)

1–2 serrano peppers, seeded (optional) and finely chopped

3 Tbsp finely chopped onions

2 Tbsp finely chopped cilantro

3 Tbsp lime juice

Kosher salt, to taste

SALSA CRUDA

3–4 tomatillos, husk removed and quartered (½ lb)

1–2 serrano peppers (divided), seeded (optional) and chopped

2 cloves garlic, peeled

1 large avocado, peeled and pitted

½ bunch cilantro, chopped

2 tsp lime juice

Kosher salt, to taste

ASSEMBLY

Beef Shank Barbacoa (see page 111)

Corn Tortillas (see here)

Roasted Tomato Salsa (see here)

Salsa Cruda (see here)

Pico de Gallo (see here)

Guacamole (see here)

La Panadería

David Cáceres and José Cáceres

BROTHERS DAVID and José Cáceres learned to bake at their mother's knee as she ran a wholesale bakery. They found youthful sales achievement by hawking her bread in Mexico City's streets and expanded those experiences into a successful family bakery in Mexico, then moved to San Antonio where their panadería became one of the city's finest Mexican artisanal bakeries.

When the Cáceres brothers made their move to San Antonio in 2013, they introduced their baked goods from a farmer's market stall, handing out samples from a basket, just as they did as kids. Their first brick and mortar proved so successful they had to double the size into the adjacent space, where La Panadería remains hopping to this day.

Unlike at other local Mexican panaderías, the brothers bake with European butter (instead of lard) and begin their breads with a twenty-year-old sourdough starter they call *el bebe*, which is fermented for forty-eight hours. These distinguishing features have added to their popularity among bread-lovers.

Not long after opening, the simple bakery evolved into a casual café, where shelves of hearty loaves of bread, delicate pastries, traditional pan dulce, and rustic seasonal treats anchor a menu of hot and cold dishes.

The brothers now proudly share the art of "Bread Cultura" at three busy cafés from downtown to the far northside, keeping their family traditions alive and thriving.

La Panadería Brioche MAKES 16 ROLLS

This recipe is made with poolish, a single-use, pre-fermented bread starter that doesn't need to be fed (unlike a sourdough). You will need to proof the dough for at least thirty hours, but it's key to a great bake. David Cáceres warns, "The biggest mistake people make is under-proofing their dough. Err on the side of too much proofing." Now you know.

POOLISH In a large bowl, mix flour, yeast, and 1¼ cups water until well incorporated. Cover with plastic wrap and ferment for at least 12 hours or overnight at room temperature, between 70°F-80°F.

BRIOCHE DOUGH In a stand mixer fitted with the hook attachment, combine flour, salt, yeast, poolish, milk, and eggs. Mix on low speed for 4 minutes. Increase to high speed and mix for 2½ minutes, until the dough is shiny and elastic.

Using the flat side of a meat mallet, pound cold butter. (This softens the butter without heating it.) With the mixer still running at high speed, gradually add sugar and cold butter for 8 minutes, until the dough is smooth and comes together.

Shape the dough into a round, folding it once or twice. Cover the bowl with a damp cloth and set aside to rise at room temperature for 1½ hours. Place the dough in a plastic container, cover with a lid or damp cloth, and refrigerate overnight or at least 12 hours.

Line 2 baking sheets with parchment paper. On a lightly floured work surface, divide the dough into 16 pieces, about 80 g each. Shape each piece into a smooth ball and divide the dough balls evenly between the baking sheets. Cover with plastic wrap or a damp towel. Refrigerate overnight.

In the morning, cover the dough with a new layer of plastic wrap and proof at room temperature (70°F-80°F) for 4-6 hours, until rolls have risen about 4 inches.

EGG WASH In a small bowl, whisk eggs and salt.

ASSEMBLY Preheat oven to 375°F. (See Note.)
Brush the tops of the rolls with egg wash. Bake for 13 minutes.

NOTE >> Dough hydration may vary with the quality and moisture content of the flour used. Baking time and temperature will vary from oven to oven.

Gold yeast requires less water and produces a quicker rise. It is recommended for sweet doughs such as this.

POOLISH
2⅓ cups bread flour
1 tsp instant dry yeast

BRIOCHE DOUGH
4½ cups bread flour, plus extra for dusting (see Note)
4¼ tsp kosher salt
1¾ tsp gold instant yeast (see Note)
Poolish (see here)
2 Tbsp whole milk
8 eggs
¾ cup (1½ sticks) cold butter, cubed
⅔ cup sugar

EGG WASH
2 eggs
Pinch of salt

ASSEMBLY
Brioche Dough (see here)
Egg Wash (see here)

Petit La Panadería
Opera Cake, p. 118–19

Petit La Panadería Opera Cake MAKES 12 PIECES

This light yet decadent pastry is layered with coffee-soaked almond cakes, French buttercream, and chocolate ganache, then topped with a chocolate glaze. Plan ahead, make it for a party, and take a bow in the spotlight.

CAKES

2½ cups almond meal

2 cups confectioners' sugar

11 eggs, 7 separated, room temperature

7 egg whites, room temperature

¼ cup sugar

1 cup cake flour

1 cup pastry flour

CHOCOLATE GANACHE

1½ cups (12 oz) couverture chocolate (58% cacao)

1¼ cups heavy cream

3 Tbsp glucose syrup

COFFEE BUTTERCREAM

2 egg whites

¾ cup sugar

1 cup (2 sticks) butter, cubed

3 Tbsp espresso coffee, room temperature

CAKES Preheat convection oven to 400°F. Line two 9- x 13-inch rimmed baking sheets with parchment paper.

Sift together almond meal and confectioners' sugar into a stand mixer. Add 4 whole eggs plus 7 egg yolks. Whip on medium-high speed until volume has doubled.

In a separate bowl, mix 14 egg whites and sugar and whip to a medium-stiff meringue. In three additions, fold meringue into the egg-almond meal mixture.

Sift cake flour and pastry flour together into a separate medium bowl. Gently and gradually fold flour into batter, taking care not to deflate batter as much as possible.

Divide batter evenly between the baking sheets, spreading it out with only a few strokes. Bake for 10–12 minutes, until cakes are slightly springy in the center. Do not overbake.

Set aside to cool in pans. Transfer cakes to racks. Wrap in plastic until ready to use. (The cakes will dry out quickly if left unwrapped.)

CHOCOLATE GANACHE Place chocolate in a medium bowl.

In a small saucepan, combine cream and syrup and bring to a boil. Pour hot mixture over chocolate, then mix well to emulsify. Press plastic wrap directly on the surface of the mixture and set aside until needed.

NOTE >> Ganache must be soft enough to spread, yet not runny. If needed, add more chocolate to thicken.

COFFEE BUTTERCREAM Combine egg whites and sugar in a bowl.

Fill a saucepan of water halfway and bring to a soft boil over medium heat. Place the bowl of egg whites and sugar over the water and whisk continuously until the mixture reaches 120°F.

Transfer the mixture to a stand mixer fitted with the whisk attachment. Whip on medium-high speed, until the volume increases and meringue has cooled to room temperature (about 70°F). Mix in butter until fully incorporated and the mixture is smooth. Add espresso and whip until smooth. Set aside.

COFFEE SOAKER In a large bowl, dissolve sugar in coffee. Stir in coffee extract. Set aside.

OPERA CAKE GLACÉ In a small saucepan, combine pâte à glacer brune and chocolate and melt over medium heat to 120°F. Stir in oil and mix well. Remove from heat and set aside at room temperature to cool. Cover and place in the refrigerator until needed.

NOTE >> Pâte à glacer brune is a dark chocolate coating made without cocoa butter, so it doesn't require tempering. It is ideal for dipping and coating and provides a glossy finish that resists hardening.

ASSEMBLY Spread a thin layer of chocolate ganache over a sheet of cake. Set aside for 2–4 hours to set.

Carefully flip cake with set ganache onto a sheet of parchment paper and then slide onto the back of a baking sheet as your working surface. The ganache side will be facing down. The ganache will not be visible, but adds a layer of texture to the cake.

Using a pastry brush, thoroughly soak cake with ¾ cup coffee soaker. Spread ½ cup coffee buttercream on top, making sure to build up the sides and corners evenly. Spread ½ cup ganache over buttercream, again making sure to build up the sides and corners evenly.

Set the next cake layer on top and soak with ¾ cup coffee soaker. Repeat the layering of buttercream and ganache as applied previously, focusing on matching the depth of the layers. Smooth top to an even finish.

Place cake in the freezer for 6–8 hours. The assembled cake at this stage can be frozen for up to a month.

In a small saucepan, reheat glacé over medium-low heat to 90°F. Place frozen cake on a rack set on a baking sheet. Pour warm glacé evenly over frozen cake.

Trim the edges to neaten cake. Using a knife dipped in warm water, cut cake into 16 even squares. Wipe the blade with a clean towel between each cut.

Use leftover ganache to pipe your initials (or any other message) on top of each slice of cake. The finished cake and slices can be refrigerated for up to 5 days. Do not refreeze the cake after glazing.

COFFEE SOAKER
2⅔ cups sugar
6½ cups strong coffee
3 Tbsp coffee extract

OPERA CAKE GLACÉ
2 cups pâte à glacer brune (see Note)
1½ cups (12 oz) couverture chocolate (64% cacao)
½ cup canola oil

ASSEMBLY
Chocolate Ganache (see here)
Cakes (see here)
Coffee Soaker (see here)
Coffee Buttercream (see here)
Opera Cake Glacé (see here)

Lala's Gorditas

Steven Pizzini

STEVEN PIZZINI comes from a long line of trailblazers. His great-great-great-grandfather Juan Seguín was an Alamo defender who helped establish Texas's independence. His family also has deep roots as pioneers of Tex-Mex cuisine: his aunt opened Teka Molino in 1938 and his father opened Taco Hut in 1958—both iconic outposts that staked the family's claim as creators of the puffy taco. Pizzini always knew he had big shoes to fill.

As the chef-owner of Lala's Gorditas, Pizzini has found ways to celebrate his heritage in his classic Tex-Mex menu. Like those before him, he preps all the vegetables, cooks all the meats, and delivers pure Tex-Mex cuisine made with love. He hand-pats every mound of authentic, artisanal *masa* (dough), made of nixtamalized corn and stone-ground on the premises using a *molino* (mill) his great-uncle Frank invented and sold in the early twentieth century. The rich gorditas are overstuffed with chicken or beef; Pizzini's signature puffy tacos are soft inside and crunchy outside, and the tender *masa* cups are filled with creamy guacamole or smooth refried beans. The recently expanded menu now includes a variety of enchiladas, seasonal soups (*caldos*), and tamales.

Pizzini reminds us that food can be a valuable form of cultural preservation. And for many locals, Lala's Gorditas is simply that—a reliable, fuss-free destination and taste memory of San Antonio authenticity and spirit.

Green Enchiladas serves 6–8

**CHICKEN STOCK AND
SHREDDED CHICKEN**

8 bone-in, skinless chicken thighs

5–6 carrots, shredded (1 lb)

1 head celery, chopped

1 onion, chopped

1 green bell pepper,
    seeded and quartered

2 Tbsp kosher salt (divided)

2 Tbsp granulated onion or
    1 Tbsp onion powder

2 Tbsp black pepper

2 tsp celery seeds, or to taste

TOMATILLO SAUCE

6 lbs tomatillos, peeled and
    thoroughly washed

3 bunches scallions, chopped

Bunch of cilantro, leaves and
    stems chopped

Chicken Stock (see here)

1 large head garlic, finely chopped
    (¼ cup)

Kosher salt, to taste

ENCHILADAS

1 cup vegetable oil

12–16 (8-inch) white corn tortillas

Shredded Chicken (see here)

Tomatillo Sauce (see here)

2 cups grated Monterey Jack cheese

Sprig of cilantro, leaves only

1 (15-oz) jar Mexican crema, to serve

Bunch of scallions, chopped,
    for garnish

CHICKEN STOCK AND SHREDDED CHICKEN In a large stockpot, bring 2 quarts water to a boil. Add chicken, carrots, celery, onions, bell peppers, and 1 tablespoon salt and bring to a boil. Boil for 1 hour, until chicken is tender and falls off the bones. Strain stock and set aside.

Transfer chicken to a cutting board, then finely shred meat. Discard vegetables.

Place chicken in a medium bowl and season with remaining 1 tablespoon salt, granulated onion (or onion powder), black pepper, and celery seeds. Toss to mix and set aside.

TOMATILLO SAUCE Place tomatillos in a large saucepan, fill with enough water to cover, and bring to a gentle boil over medium heat. Boil for 3–5 minutes, until softened. Do not crush tomatillos or allow them to crack, as this may add bitterness to the sauce.

Drain tomatillos, then transfer to a blender. Purée until smooth. Pour purée back into the saucepan. Add scallions, cilantro, and stock and bring to a gentle boil over medium heat. Stir in garlic and salt and cook for another 3 minutes. (If you boil the mixture for too long, the sauce will lose its vibrant color.) Remove from heat and set aside.

ENCHILADAS Preheat oven to 350°F.

Heat oil in a large skillet over high heat. Using tongs and averting your face from the hot oil, carefully and quickly dip a tortilla in oil to soften it.

Transfer the tortilla to a plate or cutting board. Add shredded chicken to the lower third of the tortilla and roll into a cylinder to create an enchilada. Repeat with remaining tortillas and chicken. Arrange enchiladas in a snug single layer in a 9- x 13-inch baking dish.

Cover enchiladas with sauce and top with cheese. Cover dish with aluminum foil and bake for 15 minutes, until cheese is melted. Set aside to rest for 10 minutes, then garnish with cilantro leaves.

When serving, drizzle plated enchiladas with crema and garnish with scallions.

Classic Tex-Mex Sides SERVES 8–12

You'll find rice and beans on every Tex-Mex platter. The recipes are usually passed down through generations and made with unmeasured amounts of ingredients. We've included measurements here.

SPANISH RICE Heat a medium heavy-bottomed lidded saucepan over high heat. Stir in oil and rice. Toast rice, stirring frequently to avoid burning, until light brown.

Stir in onions, garlic, and tomatoes and mix until rice is completely coated. Quickly pour in 3½ cups cold water and reduce to medium heat. Add cumin, salt, and pepper. Stir the bottom of the pan only once to prevent sticking and simmer for 10–15 minutes, until the surface of the rice is bubbling and most of the liquid has been absorbed.

Remove the pan from the heat and cover with a fitted lid. Set aside to rest for 30 minutes untouched. No peeking; otherwise, steam will be released.

FRIJOLES CHARROS In a large stockpot, combine beans, ½ onion, garlic, and salt. Fill pot with enough hot water to cover beans by double. Bring to a boil over high heat, then reduce to medium heat. Gently boil for 1½ hours, until beans are tender. (If needed, add more hot water to keep beans covered to the original level.)

About 15 minutes before beans are finished cooking, fry bacon in a large skillet over high heat until fat is rendered and bacon is soft. Chop remaining onion, then add to the skillet. Add tomatoes and jalapeño, season with a pinch of salt and pepper, and cook for 3 minutes, until onions are translucent. Stir in cilantro.

Immediately stir the bacon mixture into the pot of beans. Remove from heat and set aside to rest for at least 15 minutes. (The beans taste even better after resting in the refrigerator for a day.)

Serve with rice.

SPANISH RICE
¼ cup vegetable oil
2 cups Adolphus long-grain rice
½ onion, diced into ½-inch pieces
4–6 cloves garlic,
    peeled and crushed (2 Tbsp)
½ cup canned crushed tomatoes
1 Tbsp ground cumin
2 tsp kosher salt
1½ tsp black pepper

FRIJOLES CHARROS
3 cups dried pinto beans
1½ white or yellow onions (divided)
4–6 cloves garlic, minced (2 Tbsp)
2 Tbsp kosher salt, plus extra to taste
½ lb bacon, roughly chopped
2 tomatoes, chopped
1 jalapeño pepper, left whole
Black pepper, to taste
Bunch of cilantro, stems and
    leaves chopped
Rice, to serve

Liberty Bar

Dwight Hobart and Pedro Torres

LIBERTY BAR is a San Antonio institution with a well-earned reputation as a local favorite. In 2010, after twenty-five years in the same location, owner Dwight Hobart moved the business from a tilted 1890s saloon to a former convent now painted flamingo pink, taking its hip charm and funky vibes right along with it. Where else can you find chile relleno en nogada (a baked meat-stuffed poblano pepper topped with walnut sauce and pomegranate seeds) alongside falafel, matzo ball soup, fried calamari, and Texas panhandle beef—from the owner's ranch, no less? The menu features most everything Hobart and his extended family love to eat: handmade fettuccine with a choice of sauces, achiote-marinated chicken, baba ghanoush, old-fashioned pot roast, grilled rainbow trout with pesto, three kinds of house-baked bread, and even a side of bacon if you want it, whenever you want it. Plus pies, cakes, and fresh-churned ice cream, all overseen by Hobart and chef Pedro Torres.

The eye-catching interior décor matches the eclectic menu mash-up, with hand-painted wallpaper and antique rugs straight from an Armenian bazaar. The upstairs bar and dining area, as lively as the two dining areas downstairs, adds to the friendly ambiance with happy hours bookending the evening service schedule. It's a sure-bet experience for everyone at the table.

Buttermilk Biscuits SERVES 4–6

Dwight Hobart says this recipe can be made with buttermilk, yogurt, sour cream, or in a pinch, sweet milk with a tablespoon of lemon juice or vinegar. It calls for Crisco or lard, but you can use butter or any combination of the three. "Different ingredients will alter the texture and flavor of the dough, and you will have to adapt. That's life. Get over it," he quips.

3 Tbsp chilled Crisco or lard, cut into chunks (divided), plus extra for greasing

1¾ cups unbleached all-purpose flour, plus extra for dusting

2½ tsp baking powder

1 tsp white cane sugar

½ tsp sea salt

½ tsp baking soda

2 Tbsp chilled butter, cut into chunks (divided)

¾ cup buttermilk

NOTE >> For the tenderest biscuits, avoid kneading altogether and simply slice the flattened dough into squares or diamonds. Dough can be wrapped and refrigerated for up to 8 hours until needed.

Preheat oven to 425°F–450°F. Grease a baking sheet with Crisco (or lard), then dust with flour. Shake the sheet to even out flour, then discard any excess.

In a large bowl, combine flour, baking powder, sugar, salt, and baking soda. Whisk.

Transfer the mixture to a food processor fitted with the metal blade and pulse a few times to combine. Add half the butter and half the Crisco (or lard) to the mixture and pulse until grainy like cornmeal. Add remaining butter and Crisco and pulse a few times, until the mixture forms pea-sized clumps.

Add buttermilk and pulse three or four times, until the dough comes together as one piece. The dough should be wet enough to lump together yet dry enough to tumble with the turn of the blade. Avoid overworking the dough but be sure to incorporate all the liquid into the mixture of flour and fat. This process is known as *hydration* and is critical.

Lightly dust a cutting board or work surface with flour. Remove the dough from the processor and nudge into a single glob. With lightly dusted hands, press the dough gently with your knuckles or fingertips and flatten it out to a 1-inch thickness. (For thinner biscuits, flatten it to ½ inch.) Dip a circular cutter (a tin can with both ends removed works well) into flour, then stamp out biscuits. Using a metal spatula, lift biscuits away from the excess dough.

Gather the irregular pieces, then gently and briefly knead them together. Cut the remainder. There will always be one last dough parcel to be shaped by hand. (See Note.)

Place biscuits on the baking sheet so they're touching each other. Bake for 10–12 minutes, until biscuits are speckled brown on top and light brown on the bottom. Transfer biscuits to a rack and set aside to cool for 1–2 minutes.

When slicing them open, insert the tines of a dinner fork into the side of each biscuit, working your way around until the top separates from the bottom. (Using a knife will flatten the surface. This technique keeps them flaky and fluffy.)

Lime Chess Pie SERVES 8

PIE CRUST

2 cups unbleached all-purpose flour,
plus extra for dusting

2 tsp white cane sugar

1 tsp sea salt

¼ cup chilled Crisco (divided),
cut into chunks

2 Tbsp chilled butter (divided),
cut into chunks

1 Tbsp chilled lard (divided),
cut into chunks

5 Tbsp ice water

PIE CRUST Sift flour, sugar, and salt into a large bowl. Whisk.

Transfer the mixture to a food processor fitted with the metal blade and pulse a few times to combine. Add half each of the Crisco, butter, and lard to the mixture and pulse until grainy like cornmeal. Add remaining Crisco, butter, and lard and pulse a few times, until the mixture forms pea-sized clumps.

Add ice water and pulse three or four times, until the dough comes together as one piece. The dough should be wet enough to lump together yet dry enough to tumble with the turn of the blade. Avoid overworking the dough but be sure to incorporate all the liquid into the flour and fat mixture. This process is known as *hydration* and is critical.

Lightly dust a cutting board or work surface with flour. Remove the dough from the processor and nudge into a single glob. With lightly dusted hands, gently fold the dough onto itself a few times. You should end up with 14–16 ounces of dough. Using a sharp knife, divide into 2 equal pieces.

Gently shape the dough into two disks, each about 1–2 inches thick. (The dough will be moist, malleable, and sticky.) Wrap one piece separately in plastic wrap or wax paper and refrigerate for at least 1 hour, but preferably overnight. (This relaxes the gluten for a more pliable dough.) Tiny bubbles will speckle the surface; this is normal.

This recipe makes 2 (9-inch) crusts. Tightly wrap additional dough in aluminum foil or freezer-weight plastic wrap. Store in the refrigerator for up to 3 days or freeze for up to 6 months.

FILLING In a food processor fitted with a blade, blend eggs, sugar, and cornmeal for 1 minute. Add butter and process for another 1 minute. Add lime juice and blend for 15 seconds.

ASSEMBLY Preheat oven to 425°F.

Lightly dust a cutting board or work surface with flour. Using a rolling pin, roll out a disk of dough into an even ⅛-inch-thick layer. Line a 9-inch pie pan with the crust and use a fork to crimp the edges. Remove any excess dough with a knife.

Cover the dough with parchment paper, then fill the pan with pie weights or dry beans. Bake for 10 minutes. Carefully remove the hot weights and paper from the pan. Using a fork, prick crust a few times to release steam. Bake for another 5 minutes, until it looks dry but not necessarily cooked through. Let your conscience be your guide.

Reduce oven temperature to 350°F. Pour filling into pre-baked crust and cover any exposed crust edges with aluminum foil or parchment paper to prevent the delicate crust from burning. Bake for 50 minutes, until filling sets. Set aside at room temperature for at least 1 hour.

Serve.

FILLING
6 eggs
2 cups sugar
2 Tbsp cornmeal
¾ cup (1½ sticks) butter,
    room temperature
¾ cup lime juice

ASSEMBLY
Unbleached all-purpose flour,
    for dusting
1 Pie Crust (see here)
Filling (see here)

Little Gretel
Denise Mazal

THE EUROPEAN history steeped into the dishes at this charming destination is as rich as the sauces on the plates. The riverside space in Boerne fits Czech-born chef-owner Denise Mazal to a tee. The décor, sprinkled with reminders of the arts and crafts of Germany, Austria, Hungary, and the Czech Republic, celebrates her home region.

Mazal developed her culinary passion watching her mother cook in restaurant kitchens in Prague. Mazal remains deeply immersed in the food traditions of her native land. After defecting in the mid-1970s at the height of the struggles between communism and democracy, she now returns annually to deepen her culinary knowledge by working alongside other Czech chefs. She reciprocates by hosting the same chefs when they visit Texas for long runs of special game dinners at Little Gretel.

Most impressively, nearly everything on the menu is prepared from scratch: sweet and savory Czech *kolaches* (sweet fruit-filled pastries), oven-finished schnitzels, 72-hour braised *sauerbraten* (beef stew), and wild game cooked on outdoor grills and smokers. The result is a mix of small-town café, home kitchen, and national pride.

Ricotta Dumplings with Seasonal Fruit Sauce SERVES 6

Czechs enjoy sweet dumplings not only as desserts but also as entrées. These dumplings take advantage of bountiful seasonal fruit such as strawberries from March to April, peaches and apricots from May to June, and sugar plums and berries in July and August.

RICOTTA DUMPLINGS In a large bowl, combine Wondra flour, semolina flour, sugar, 1 teaspoon salt, ricotta, egg yolks, and melted butter. Using your hands, combine ingredients to form a smooth dough. Do not overwork the dough.

Place the dough onto a lightly floured board and divide into 2 equal pieces. Form into round cylindrical loaves, each 2 inches in height. Rest in the refrigerator, covered, for 20 minutes.

Meanwhile, bring a large saucepan of water and the remaining 1 teaspoon salt to a boil.

Slice each loaf into 12 equal pieces and roll each piece into a smooth ball, making sure to close the seams.

Reduce the saucepan to medium heat. Carefully lower in dumplings and stir immediately to prevent them from sticking to the bottom of the pan. Cook for 8–10 minutes, until dumplings float to the surface. To check for doneness, transfer a dumpling to a cutting board and cut in half using a long piece of sewing thread. If the dough is still raw on the inside, cook dumplings for another few minutes. (Make a note of the boiling time for when you next make the recipe.)

Using a slotted spoon, transfer dumplings to a large tray. Cover to keep warm and moist.

SEASONAL FRUIT SAUCE Melt butter in a skillet over low heat. Add sugar and cinnamon and stir to melt sugar. Add fruit and cook gently for 5 minutes, until warmed through and coated with butter. Stir in lemon juice.

ASSEMBLY Place equal amounts of warm dumplings on 6 plates. Spoon hot fruit sauce around and over dumplings and top with whipped cream. Finish with a sprinkle of sugar and sprig of mint (if using).

RICOTTA DUMPLINGS
1¼ cups Wondra flour, plus extra for dusting
¼ cup semolina flour
¼ cup confectioners' sugar
2 tsp kosher salt (divided)
2 cups whole-milk ricotta, drained
3 egg yolks
⅓ cup butter, melted

SEASONAL FRUIT SAUCE
¼ cup (½ stick) butter
1 Tbsp sugar
1 tsp ground cinnamon
3 cups mixed seasonal fruit
1 tsp lemon juice

ASSEMBLY
Ricotta Dumplings (see here)
Seasonal Fruit Sauce (see here)
Whipped cream
¼ cup confectioners' sugar (optional)
Sprigs of mint (optional)

Chicken Paprika with Czech Bread Dumplings SERVES 4

Paprika introduces a distinct sweetness to this comforting dish. The bread dumplings accompanying it are unique to Czech cuisine. You'll want to plan ahead: the bread needs to be dried for three days before starting the dumpling recipe.

CZECH BREAD DUMPLINGS

3½ cups + 1 Tbsp warm milk (no warmer than 110°F)

¼ cup active dry yeast

1 Tbsp sugar

7 cups Wondra flour

1½ Tbsp kosher salt

¼ cup vegetable oil

2 eggs

½ loaf white bread, cut into ½-inch cubes and dried for 3 days at room temperature

Spray bottle of vegetable oil

CHICKEN PAPRIKA

1 (4-lb) whole chicken

3 Tbsp butter

1 yellow onion, sliced (1 cup)

3 Tbsp paprika

1 Tbsp kosher salt, plus more to taste

3 cups chicken stock

1 cup cold half-and-half

¼ cup all-purpose flour

CZECH BREAD DUMPLINGS Preheat oven to 350°F.

In a bowl, combine milk, yeast, and sugar and stir.

In a stand mixer fitted with the hook attachment, combine flour, salt, oil, and eggs and mix well. Add the yeast mixture and mix on slow speed for 4–5 minutes.

Meanwhile, place cubed bread on a baking sheet. Spray with oil and toast in the oven for 6 minutes. Fold croutons into the dough mixture. Cover with a dish towel or plastic wrap. Set aside at room temperature for 2 hours, until doubled in size.

CHICKEN PAPRIKA Remove the spine from chicken and discard. Cut chicken into quarters.

In a large Dutch oven, melt butter over medium-high heat. Add onions and sauté for 3–5 minutes, until light golden brown. Stir in paprika and salt. Slowly pour in stock and add chicken. Bring to a gentle boil over high heat, then reduce to medium heat and simmer for 30 minutes. Using a slotted spoon, transfer chicken to a cutting board and set aside.

In a small bowl, combine half-and-half and flour and mix well. Add the mixture to the sauce, then blend with an immersion blender. Cook for another 8–10 minutes, until thickened. Season with salt.

Return chicken to sauce and keep warm.

ASSEMBLY Grease a baking sheet.

Divide the bread dumpling dough evenly into 4 balls and set them on the baking sheet. Set aside for 10 minutes to rise.

Roll each ball into a 2-inch-thick log and place on the baking sheet to rise again for 10 minutes.

In a large double boiler, bring water to a boil. Place dumplings into the steamer and cook for 9–10 minutes. (Depending on the size of your steamer, you may have to work in batches.) Turn them over and cook for another 9–10 minutes, until steamed through. To check for doneness, remove a dough log and cut in half using a long piece of sewing thread. If the dough is still raw on the inside, cook for another few minutes. (Make a note of the steaming time for when you next make the recipe.)

Transfer dumplings to a large tray. Using a fork, pierce holes in the top to release the steam. Set aside to cool.

Slice dumplings into ½-inch-thick slices and steam again until they look and feel slippery, using a spray of oil to keep them moist. Unused dumplings can be well wrapped and stored in the refrigerator for up to 4 days or wrapped and frozen for up to 6 months.

To serve, thaw first, if needed, and re-steam. Place a portion of chicken on a plate and ladle sauce on top. Arrange three slices of steamed dumplings next to chicken. Top chicken with a dollop of sour cream and a floret of parsley.

ASSEMBLY

Spray bottle of vegetable oil,
  for greasing
Czech Bread Dumplings (see here)
Chicken Paprika (see here)
⅓ cup sour cream, for garnish
Sprig of curly parsley, for garnish

Mama's Café
Gabriel Ibarra

CAPPY LAWTON and his former partners opened a Mama's Café in this spot and several others around town in 1981, then he sold his share of the business in 1988 to concentrate on other projects. Nearly thirty-five years later, his Lawton Family of Restaurants group reclaimed the space and returned high-quality comfort food to the tables. Chef Gabriel Ibarra oversees the culinary activities for the entire restaurant group, including the Mama's kitchen.

Texas roadhouse staples—chicken-fried steak, meatloaf, liver and onions, chili, and burgers—are now made with top-rated, grass-fed, local beef in a scratch kitchen. Throwback favorites including the quirky McQueeney Special (a crunchy iceberg lettuce salad topped with corn chips, cheddar, and house chili) and the Chicken Melt (a plump, juicy breast topped with melted cheddar and avocado) have returned better than ever. Even the uber-popular fried mushrooms seem peppier and more flavorful.

The décor is much improved, too. The dining room is dominated by a pointillism-inspired bottlecap portrait of Willie Nelson (created by Cappy's artistic brother Brad) and adorned in old cowboy boots, hats, and branding irons. The oak-canopied courtyard features colorful tile tabletops and a trickling fountain. None of it comes off as forced, either. This restaurant is a labor of love, from the warm greeting to the desserts. Old-timers have returned with fond memories revived, seated beside fresh faces who are all delighted to discover a genuine Texan culinary experience.

MAMA'S CAFÉ Southern Cornbread, p. 138 and Mama's Texas Chili, p. 139

Southern Cornbread SERVES 8–10

Sure, cornbread is great with chili. But it's also delicious on its own, griddled and slathered with butter, or even crumbled into soup. It's an easy substitution for dinner rolls (and much quicker to master).

¾ cup (1½ sticks) butter, melted and cooled to room temperature, plus extra for greasing

5 cups cornmeal

1 cup gluten-free flour (preferably Bob's Red Mill)

1 cup sugar

2 Tbsp baking soda

2 Tbsp baking powder

½ tsp kosher salt

6 cups buttermilk

½ cup sour cream

6 eggs

Preheat oven to 350°F. If baking in a convection oven, use a low fan. Grease the bottom and sides of an 18- x 13-inch rimmed baking sheet with butter.

In a large bowl, combine cornmeal, flour, sugar, baking soda, baking powder, and salt and mix well.

In a separate bowl, combine melted butter, buttermilk, sour cream, and eggs and mix thoroughly. Add wet ingredients to dry ingredients and mix well.

Carefully pour batter into the baking sheet and spread it out evenly. Bake for 25–30 minutes, until a toothpick inserted in the middle comes out clean and relatively dry. Set aside to cool, then serve.

Mama's Texas Chili SERVES 6

Seeing this iconic one-pot meal is a sure sign you're in Texas—especially if it's free of beans, as this one is.

In a large Dutch oven, heat 1 tablespoon oil over medium-high heat. Season meats with 1 tablespoon oregano, 1 tablespoon cumin, salt, and black pepper. Working in batches, add meat to the Dutch oven in a single layer. Sear for 5 minutes, turning, until lightly browned on all sides. Using a slotted spoon, transfer meat to a platter.

With the Dutch oven still over medium-high heat, and all the caramelized bits still coating the bottom, heat remaining 1 tablespoon oil. Add onions and sauté for 3 minutes, until translucent. Add garlic, remaining 1 teaspoon oregano and cumin, ancho chiles, guajillo chiles, chiles de arbol, and flour. Stir continuously for 1 minute to toast seasonings and cook flour.

Add stock and vinegar and stir to incorporate. Add meats, reduce to medium-low heat, and gently simmer for 45 minutes to 1 hour, until meat is tender.

TO SERVE Ladle chili into large cups or bowls and serve with a generous portion of cornbread. Top with your favorite toppings.

2 Tbsp canola oil (divided)

2 lbs pork butt or pork stew meat, trimmed and diced into 1-inch pieces

2 lbs beef chuck roast, trimmed and diced into 1-inch pieces

1 Tbsp + 1 tsp dried oregano (divided)

1 Tbsp + 1 tsp ground cumin (divided)

2 Tbsp kosher salt

1 tsp black pepper

2 onions, chopped

2–3 cloves garlic, minced

6 ancho chiles, seeded, roasted, and finely ground

4 guajillo chiles, seeded, roasted, and finely ground

2 chiles de arbol, seeded, roasted, and finely ground

¼ cup gluten-free flour (preferably Bob's Red Mill)

2 qts no- or low-sodium beef stock

¼ cup apple cider vinegar

TO SERVE
Southern Cornbread (see page 138)
Cheddar
Sour cream
Chopped scallions
Fritos Chili Cheese Corn Chips

Maverick
Texas Brasserie

Chris Carlson

OPENED IN early 2018, Maverick feels like it's been around for decades. The seasoned, unpretentious front-of-house team understands how to extend a warm welcome, the bartenders stir and shake well-balanced booze, the wine list accents the menu, and the kitchen staff sure knows how to cook.

The menu's steel-eyed focus is on Texas ingredients treated with continental flair. Share-friendly plates include classic beef tartare and gnocchi with goat cheese crème fraîche. Mains such as pork schnitzel with lemon, capers, and brown butter, confit half duck, and pan-seared trout almondine are nothing short of impressive. The steak entrées change with availability, as does the daily seasonal fish selection from the Gulf Coast. And although the à la carte options dominate the menu, the three-course Plats Du Jour urges serious consideration. From beef bourguignon and porchetta to coq au vin, the daily special entrée invites you to choose your dining schedule.

Black lacquered cane-back chairs, banquette seating, low-back bar stools, and Edison bulbs lend a vintage-modern vibe to the main dining areas. At the same time, the patio maintains a year-round temperature with fans, misters, and heaters. It's all in support of guest comfort and happiness that keeps neighbors walking in and visitors enthralled.

Cauliflower Curry Bowls SERVES 4

CURRIED CAULIFLOWER PURÉE

1 large head cauliflower,
   cored and quartered
4 cups whole milk
1 cup (2 sticks) butter,
   room temperature
3 Tbsp yellow curry paste
3 tsp ground turmeric
3 tsp curry powder
Kosher salt and black pepper, to taste

ROASTED CAULIFLOWER

1 large head cauliflower
Vegetable oil, for brushing
Kosher salt and black pepper

PICKLED RAISINS

5 star anise
1 cup golden raisins
1 cup sugar
1 Tbsp kosher salt
1 cup distilled white vinegar

ASSEMBLY

Curried Cauliflower Purée (see here)
Roasted Cauliflower (see here)
Pickled Raisins (see here), for garnish
3 oz Marcona almonds, toasted,
   for garnish
½ bunch Italian parsley, chopped,
   for garnish

CURRIED CAULIFLOWER PURÉE Place cauliflower in a deep saucepan. Cover with milk, topping up with water if necessary. Cut a circle of parchment paper and place it on the surface of the liquid. Cook slowly over low heat for 45 minutes, until cauliflower is tender.

Drain, then transfer cauliflower to a food processor or blender. Add remaining ingredients and purée. Set aside.

ROASTED CAULIFLOWER Preheat oven to 300°F. Line a baking sheet with parchment paper.

Slice cauliflower into ½-inch "steaks" and place on the baking sheet in a single layer. Generously brush both sides of cauliflower with oil, then season with salt and pepper. Roast for 40 minutes, until golden brown and cooked through. Set aside.

PICKLED RAISINS In a small saucepan, combine all ingredients and add 1 cup water. Simmer over medium heat for 5 minutes. Set aside to cool to room temperature.

ASSEMBLY Divide purée among 4 shallow bowls. Place a slice of roasted cauliflower on top of purée, then garnish with pickled raisins, almonds, and parsley.

Calamari and Octopus SERVES 2

An exciting exploration in textural contrasts, this showy dish is sure to thrill any seafood lover. Note: This recipe requires a sous-vide circulator and vacuum-sealed bags.

OCTOPUS Vacuum-seal all ingredients in a bag and circulate at 180°F (82°C) for 4 hours. Remove from water and chill in an ice bath.

CALAMARI Combine calamari and egg whites in a bowl. Cover and refrigerate for at least 4 hours.

FINGERLING POTATOES Put potatoes in a saucepan and fill with enough water to cover. Add salt and cook on medium-high heat for 20 minutes, until fork tender. Do not overcook. Drain, then set aside to cool to room temperature.

Slice in half lengthwise.

ASSEMBLY In a skillet, heat vegetable oil over medium-high heat. Add potatoes and sauté for 3 minutes, until crisp. Add garlic, Calabrese peppers, and rosemary and stir to combine. Discard rosemary stem. Divide the mixture between 2 plates.

Preheat a grill pan over medium-high heat.

Add octopus to the grill and grill for 2–3 minutes total, until heated through and grill marks form.

In a deep skillet, heat 2 inches of vegetable oil to 350°F. Put flour in a bowl. Drain calamari, then add to flour and toss. Tap off excess flour, then carefully, averting your face from the hot oil, lower calamari into oil and fry for 4 minutes total, until crisp and golden brown. Using a slotted spoon, transfer to a paper towel–lined plate to drain. Lightly season with salt and pepper.

Slice grilled octopus and arrange over the potato mixture. Top with fried calamari, a drizzle of Calabrian oil, and a sprinkle of paprika. Garnish with scallions and parsley.

OCTOPUS
8 oz octopus tentacles
3 cloves garlic, peeled
2 Calabrese peppers
Sprig of rosemary
2 Tbsp Calabrian chili oil
   (available in gourmet grocery
   stores)

CALAMARI
8 oz calamari, sliced into
   ½-inch ribbons
6 egg whites

FINGERLING POTATOES
6 oz fingerling potatoes
1 tsp kosher salt

ASSEMBLY
1 Tbsp vegetable oil, plus extra
   for deep-frying
Fingerling Potatoes (see here)
3 cloves garlic, peeled
3 Calabrese peppers, sliced
Sprig of rosemary
Octopus (see here)
2 cups all-purpose flour
Calamari (see here)
Kosher salt and black pepper, to taste
Calabrian chili oil, for drizzling
Smoked paprika, for sprinkling
Bunch of scallions, sliced, for garnish
½ bunch Italian parsley, chopped,
   for garnish

Max & Louie's New York Diner

Drew Glick

WHEN LONG Islanders Drew and Wendy Glick moved to San Antonio in 2011 to open their first restaurant, the thing they missed most from home was family dinners at their local diner. San Antonio lacked anything resembling an East Coast diner, so when the Glicks had the opportunity, they switched gears and opened Max & Louie's New York Diner in 2016. And it was an instant hit.

There's a vast menu to choose from: scratch pancakes, waffles, and fluffy omelets lead an all-day breakfast menu; lunchtime sandwiches are super-stacked with corned beef, pastrami, and turkey; and diner classics such as burgers, chops, and handspun milkshakes are always popular. There's a definite Jewish deli vibe, too, with sell-out baskets of house-made bagels, chicken matzo ball soup, cheese blintzes, and chocolate babka. And to round it all off, New York–style cheesecake and mile-high layer cakes.

The restaurant has doubled in size since opening, even weathering the COVID lockdown with takeout and delivery. And when Max & Louie's reopened, they ensured ample distancing and branded dividers between booths. The crowds barely stopped ordering. The friendly staff and the owners' hands-on style have created an inviting atmosphere for Texas families who, just like the Glicks, will now have fond memories of family meals at their local diner.

Bubbe Ray's Split Pea Soup SERVES 8

This comforting and reliable soup, courtesy of an heirloom recipe, is on regular rotation at the diner. Owner Drew Glick says, "The flavorful, hearty soup will leave you feeling as warm as a loving hug from your grandmother." Serve it with crusty rye bread for a nourishing and satisfying home-cooked meal.

Bring peas and 3½ quarts water to a boil in a stockpot. Reduce to low heat and simmer, uncovered, for 1 hour. Skim off any foam.

Add vegetables and chicken bouillon (if using) and simmer for 1½ hours.

Season with salt, sugar, and pepper and stir. Set aside to cool for 10–15 minutes.

Using an immersion blender, blend until smooth.

1 lb dried split peas, rinsed
6 stalks celery, chopped
5–6 carrots (1 lb), peeled and sliced into rounds
2 yellow onions, chopped
2 zucchinis, sliced
2 yellow squash, sliced
1 medium sweet potato (½ lb), peeled and chopped
1 cube chicken bouillon (optional)
2½ tsp kosher salt
1 tsp sugar
½ tsp black pepper

Stuffed Cabbage in Sweet and Sour Sauce SERVES 8

Stuffed cabbage has two-thousand-year-old roots in Eastern European Jewish tradition. This version with the sweet and sour sauce is served in homes for the fall and winter holidays, and in authentic Jewish diners and delis around the world.

SWEET AND SOUR SAUCE Heat oil in a medium saucepan over medium heat. Add onions and sauté for 5 minutes, until translucent. Stir in tomato paste and cook for 3 minutes. Add sugar, raisins, salt, and pepper and stir until sugar has dissolved. Stir in tomatoes and ketchup, then simmer for 20–30 minutes.

Remove from heat and stir in vinegar. Mix well and set aside.

CABBAGE ROLLS Using a paring knife, core the cabbage.

In a large steamer pot with a removable basket, steam cabbage, cut side down, at medium-high heat for 15 minutes. Carefully remove cabbage and set aside until cool to the touch.

Gently peel off whole cabbage leaves, one by one, and set aside to drain. You'll need 16 large leaves.

In a large bowl, use your hands to gently fold together remaining ingredients.

Lay a cabbage leaf with the core side toward you. Pinch off about ¼ cup of the meat mixture and shape it into a log in the cup of the cabbage leaf. The amount of meat depends on the size of the leaf, so adjust accordingly. Roll the cabbage over the meat mixture, tucking in the sides to create a sealed roll. Place the roll, seam side down, on a baking sheet. Repeat with remaining cabbage leaves.

ASSEMBLY Preheat oven to 350°F.

Ladle 1 cup of sauce into a 13- x 9-inch baking dish and spread over the bottom surface. Place stuffed cabbage rolls, seam side down, into the dish, snug against each other. Ladle remaining sauce over cabbage rolls. (You may need to use an additional 8-inch square dish if you have an abundance of rolls.) Cover with aluminum foil and bake for 1 hour.

Serve cabbage rolls on top of mashed potatoes (or egg noodles or rice) with additional warm sauce from the baking dish.

SWEET AND SOUR SAUCE

2 tsp canola oil
1 small yellow onion, chopped
6 Tbsp tomato paste
½ cup brown sugar
½ cup golden raisins
1½ tsp kosher salt
1½ tsp black pepper
4 cups canned crushed tomatoes
1 cup ketchup
½ cup red wine vinegar

CABBAGE ROLLS

1 head cabbage
2 lbs ground beef
1 cup uncooked parboiled rice
   (preferably Ben's Original)
2 onions, finely chopped
2 cloves garlic, minced
1 egg, beaten
1½ Tbsp kosher salt
1½ tsp black pepper

ASSEMBLY

Sweet and Sour Sauce (see here)
Cabbage Rolls (see here)
Mashed potatoes, egg noodles,
   or rice, to serve

Meadow
PJ Edwards

CHEF PJ EDWARDS and his wife, Lindsey, opened Meadow in 2018 after years of working at other restaurants. It's been a strong start for this charming couple, whose menu and hospitality are knocking it out of the park.

Local, seasonal ingredients take center stage in PJ's Texas/Southern cooking, and the varied menu features creative plant-forward dishes that showcase the chef's love of root-to-stem cooking. English pea hummus is herbaceous and smooth, while a cabbage pancake topped with a fried egg and sweet red cabbage syrup puts other vegetable sides to shame. PJ's deft handiwork even shows up in the turmeric-tinged Chow-Chow Relish and in the don't-miss jar of seasonal pickles. Rest assured the meat dishes are equal contenders: brisket takes a bow alongside the noteworthy fried chicken and a tall two-fisted burger.

Meadow touts itself as a neighborhood eatery for good reason. Good food is the cornerstone of most successful restaurants, but the Edwardses also recognize the value of guest experience. Lindsey leads a front-of-house team committed to service, and her warm welcomes and attentive service show off Southern hospitality at its best. All this in a modern rustic dining space with a tree-covered patio retreat—it's no surprise that Meadow has become a Sunday brunch hotspot for slow sips of mimosas and hearty-yet-healthy, day-starting meals.

Cast-Iron Cornbread with Jalapeño-Pimento Cheese and Honey-Lard Butter SERVES 6-8

When served with pimento cheese and honey-lard butter, this cornbread has its bona fide Southern roots on proud display.

JALAPEÑO-PIMENTO CHEESE

2 cups shredded cheddar

¼ cup Duke's Mayonnaise

¼ cup cream cheese, room temperature

1 Tbsp finely chopped piquillo peppers

1 Tbsp pickled jalapeño juice

5 dashes Crystal or your favorite hot sauce

1 tsp finely chopped pickled jalapeño peppers

2 tsp kosher salt

1 tsp smoked paprika

½ tsp onion powder

¼ tsp garlic powder

HONEY-LARD BUTTER

½ cup (1 stick) butter, softened

½ cup lard or rendered bacon fat

2 Tbsp honey

1 tsp coarse sea salt

CORNBREAD

4 cups high-quality cornmeal

1 Tbsp kosher salt

1 Tbsp baking powder

1 tsp baking soda

1 tsp black pepper

2 eggs

3 cups buttermilk, plus extra if needed

1 cup (2 sticks) butter, melted (divided)

JALAPEÑO-PIMENTO CHEESE Combine all ingredients in a medium bowl. While wearing plastic gloves, mix thoroughly with your hands. (Mixing with your hands will help incorporate cheese into other ingredients.)

Place in a serving bowl and serve at room temperature. Leftover cheese can be stored in the refrigerator for up to a week. Bring to room temperature before serving.

HONEY-LARD BUTTER In a stand mixer fitted with the paddle attachment, combine all ingredients and whip until smooth. Makes 2 cups.

Leftover honey-lard butter can be stored in the refrigerator for 2 weeks. Bring to room temperature before serving.

CORNBREAD Preheat oven to 400°F. Place an 8-inch cast-iron skillet in the oven for at least 10 minutes. This is an important step to ensuring a seared, sturdy crust.

Meanwhile, prepare the batter. In a medium bowl, mix cornmeal, salt, baking powder, baking soda, and pepper.

In a separate bowl, mix eggs and buttermilk. Pour wet mixture into dry mixture and whisk until smooth. Add ½ cup (1 stick) melted butter to batter and whisk until fully incorporated. If batter is too dry or stiff, whisk in another ¼ cup buttermilk.

Remove the skillet from the oven. Add remaining ½ cup (1 stick) melted butter to the skillet and swirl to coat. Add batter. A crust will start to form on the outer edges of the cornbread almost immediately. Bake in the skillet for 45 minutes, until a skewer inserted into the center comes out clean. Set aside to rest for 10 minutes.

ASSEMBLY Carefully flip the cornbread from the skillet onto a large dinner plate. Slice and serve alongside jalapeño-pimento cheese and honey-lard butter.

Fried Chicken SERVES 2–4

This dairy-free fried chicken is deep-fried at a high temperature for the requisite crispy crunch.

CHICKEN SPICE In a bowl, combine all ingredients and mix well. Leftover spice mix can be stored in an airtight container or spice shaker for up to a month.

MARINATED CHICKEN Place chicken in a large bowl. Add remaining ingredients and mix thoroughly to coat each piece. Cover tightly and refrigerate for at least 12 hours.

BATTER Combine all ingredients in a large bowl. Add 1¾ cups cool water and whisk until smooth.

FRIED CHICKEN Heat oil in a deep fryer or deep saucepan to a temperature of 375°F.

Remove chicken from marinade. Allow moisture to drip off the pieces, then drench them in batter. If preparing chicken in advance, soak chicken in batter and refrigerate for up to 2 hours.

Working in batches to avoid overcrowding and averting your face from the hot oil, carefully lower chicken into oil, one piece at a time. Do your best to keep the pieces apart to prevent them from sticking together. Using tongs, separate pieces as they cook to ensure crispness. Deep-fry for 12–15 minutes, until chicken reaches an internal temperature of 170°F. Using a slotted spoon, carefully transfer chicken to a paper towel–lined plate to drain. Repeat with remaining chicken pieces, ensuring the oil temperature remains constant at 375°F.

ASSEMBLY Dust fried chicken with a generous sprinkling of chicken spice. Serve with hot sauce and pickled vegetables.

CHICKEN SPICE
1 Tbsp fine sea salt
1 tsp black pepper
1 tsp smoked paprika
1 tsp onion powder
1 tsp garlic powder
1 tsp dried Mexican oregano
1 tsp Spanish paprika
½ tsp mustard powder
½ tsp cayenne pepper

MARINATED CHICKEN
1 (3½-lb) whole chicken, cut into
    2 wings, 2 boneless breasts,
    2 bone-in thighs, and 2 drumsticks
2 Tbsp Chicken Spice (see here)
¼ cup tamari or soy sauce
2 Tbsp hot sauce (preferably Crystal)

BATTER
1 cup all-purpose flour
¾ cup cornstarch
¼ cup rice flour

FRIED CHICKEN
Neutral oil such as canola,
    for deep-frying
Marinated Chicken (see here)
Batter (see here)

ASSEMBLY
Fried Chicken (see here)
Chicken Spice (see here),
    for sprinkling
Hot sauce, to serve
Pickled vegetables, to serve

Mi Tierra
Café y Panadería
Raul Salazar

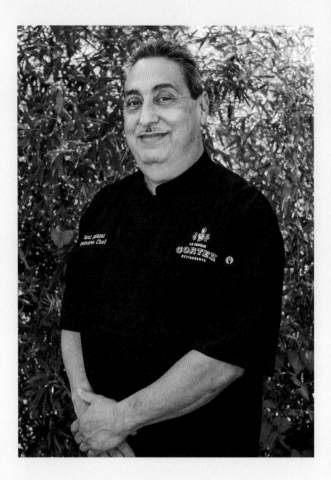

FOUNDED IN 1941, Mi Tierra Café y Panadería in Market Square has been an integral part of raising the profile and preserving the history of San Antonio's Tex-Mex cuisine. Its founding family, descendants of Pedro and Cruz Cortez, still own and operate the flagship Mi Tierra and an armada of other restaurants (La Margarita, Pico de Gallo, Viva Villa, and Mi Familia at the Rim).

For generations of locals, Mi Tierra has been the go-to after prom, before and after Fiesta parades and parties, and for late-night snacks. A business doesn't remain this popular without good food. The enormous picture book of a menu features everything from all-day breakfast to nightcap cocktails, but it's the Tex-Mex favorites—enchiladas, flautas, sizzling fajitas, tostadas, and breakfast tacos—that represent the city's unique cuisine. There's even roasted *cabrito* (goat), a rarity on menus, and tamales topped with chili.

Unfazed by passing trays of hot food, mariachi trios roam the dining room with the music almost as loud as the over-the-top décor. Diners are drawn (and rightfully so) to a massive, well-stocked case of Mexican pan dulce and candies. It's part of the bustle that places Mi Tierra on everyone's "must do when in San Antonio" list.

Classic Chili con Carne SERVES 4–6

This recipe has been handed down through the Cortez family for generations. The layers of natural flavor in this chili con carne are reminiscent of the heady stew cooked in kettles by San Antonio's famous Chili Queens in the 1800s. Their stalls were set up near the present-day Market Square, where Mi Tierra now stands.

ANCHO CHILE PURÉE Place chiles in a medium saucepan and cover with water. Weigh down chiles with a heatproof plate to keep them submerged in the water. Bring water to a simmer over medium heat and cook for 15 minutes, until chiles are soft and pliable. Drain and discard water.

Working over the sink, tear each chile open with your hands (see Note). Remove seeds, stem, and ribs. Rinse, then transfer chiles to a blender. Add 1½ cups water and blend until smooth. Set aside.

NOTE >> If you have sensitive skin, wear gloves while cleaning the chiles. Leftover purée can be poured into an ice-cube tray and frozen for future use.

CHILI Melt lard in a large saucepan or Dutch oven over medium heat. Add beef in a single layer and sear for 5 minutes total on all sides. Sprinkle in masa, mix to coat beef, and cook for another minute.

Add remaining ingredients and 3 cups water. Bring to a boil, then reduce to low heat and simmer for 20 minutes, until slightly thickened.

Note: For a deeper flavor, refrigerate chili overnight.

TO SERVE Ladle chili into large bowls and add your preferred garnishes.

ANCHO CHILE PURÉE
12 ancho chiles

CHILI
3 Tbsp lard
2 lbs boneless chuck beef, cut into 1½-inch strips
2 Tbsp masa harina (corn masa flour, preferably Maseca)
2 bay leaves
2 cloves garlic, minced
1½ cups Ancho Chile Purée (see here)
3 Tbsp chicken base (preferably Knorr)
1 tsp dried Mexican oregano
½ tsp ground cumin
¼ tsp kosher salt, plus extra to taste

TO SERVE
Shredded aged cheddar
Sliced scallions
Fresh jalapeño slices
Chopped white onion
Sliced avocado
Soft corn tortillas
Crispy tostadas

Tex-Mex Chilaquiles SERVES 4–6

What's the best thing about Tex-Mex chilaquiles? They contain scrambled eggs, so the dish can be enjoyed at breakfast, brunch, lunch, and yes, even dinner.

SALSA RANCHERA Place tomatoes in a large saucepan and cover with water. Bring to a boil, then reduce to medium-low heat and simmer for 10 minutes, until softened.

Transfer tomatoes and water into a blender. Add remaining ingredients and pulse until blended but slightly chunky. Transfer the mixture to the pan and simmer for 10 minutes, stirring often. Season with more salt. Set aside.

Leftover salsa can be stored in an airtight container for up to a week. It can be used over enchiladas, grilled chicken, or steak (and as a chip dip).

CHILAQUILES Preheat oven to 350°F.

Heat oil in a large nonstick skillet over medium heat. Add tortilla chips and toast slightly for 20 seconds. Add eggs, stir, and cook for 2 minutes, until softly scrambled.

Transfer the mixture to a casserole dish and spread into a single layer. Ladle salsa evenly over eggs, then top with both cheeses. Bake for 5 minutes, until cheese has melted.

Serve with warm tortillas and remaining salsa ranchera.

SALSA RANCHERA
2 lbs tomatoes
3 cloves garlic, minced
4 scallions, chopped into ½-inch pieces (½ cup)
1 onion, chopped (½ cup)
1 jalapeño pepper, seeded (optional) and chopped
1 (14½-oz) can fire-roasted crushed tomatoes
1 Tbsp tomato paste
1 Tbsp kosher salt, plus extra to taste

CHILAQUILES
1 Tbsp vegetable oil
20–30 thick-cut tortilla chips, broken into 1-inch pieces (1½ cups)
8 eggs, lightly beaten
2 cups Salsa Ranchera (see here), plus extra to serve
½ cup shredded Monterey Jack
½ cup shredded aged cheddar
Warm tortillas, to serve

Ming's
Ming Qian von Bargen

IN 2011, lines never let up at Ming's Thing, the farmer's market stall where chef Ming Qian von Bargen first introduced her creative Beijing street food through handcrafted sausages, crêpes, noodles, and overstuffed bao buns. Soon, she was busy catering and overseeing her inaugural restaurant, Ming's Noodle Bar, set in a converted rail car near her catering kitchen. Eventually, she outgrew the tiny space and moved to a bigger and brighter building with a new restaurant and name—Ming's. Now, there's plenty of elbow room inside and on the spacious patio.

The expanded restaurant menu also allows the chef to spread her wings. Here, you'll find a variety of hot and chilled noodle dishes with meats, tofu, and veggies, savory curried rice bowls, and restorative noodle soups. Ming's also offers many of the signature steamed buns made popular at the farmer's market—the Sloopy Bun, for example, is a delightful mix of Chinese-spiced hand-pulled pork shoulder, carrots, scallions, and a perky ginger dressing piled into a bao bun. Behind the walk-up order counter, the tempting beer selection and frozen sake cocktail spinners are in full view for a new boost of mealtime delight.

Stewed Beef with Potatoes SERVES 6

Heat oil in a Dutch oven over medium heat. Add beef and cook for 3-4 minutes, until opaque on all sides. Add sugar and cook for another 2-3 minutes. Stir in ginger and scallions and sauté for 2-3 minutes, until aromatic.

Add soy sauce, dark soy sauce, wine, star anise, and enough water to cover the meat by ½ inch. Cover tightly with a lid and simmer over low heat for 1 hour, until meat is tender.

Add potatoes and bring to a boil. Reduce to a simmer for 10 minutes, until potatoes are tender.

TO SERVE Transfer stew to a serving platter or shallow bowl and garnish with scallions. Serve with rice.

¼ cup vegetable oil

3 lbs beef shoulder, diced into 1½-2-inch cubes

¼ cup brown sugar

1 thumb-sized piece ginger, thickly sliced

4 scallions, cut into 1-inch pieces

1 cup soy sauce

6 Tbsp dark soy sauce

2 Tbsp Shaoxing rice wine

3 star anise

2 lbs yellow potatoes, cut into 1-inch cubes

TO SERVE

5 scallion greens, finely chopped, for garnish

White rice

Pearl Dumplings MAKES 25–30

PEARL DUMPLINGS Set rice aside in a fine-mesh sieve to drain thoroughly.

Combine remaining ingredients in a large bowl and mix well.

Check seasoning by cooking a teaspoon of the mixture in a small skillet over medium heat, then adjust for salt as needed.

Roll raw meat mixture into balls, about 1 inch each in diameter. Roll the meatballs in the top layer of rice in the sieve. This will ensure you are using the driest grains as you proceed.

Prepare 2 (10-inch) stackable bamboo steamers over boiling water. (Bamboo steamers are available in most Asian supermarkets.) Arrange dumplings in the steamer baskets, evenly spacing them ½ inch apart so rice can expand. Steam on medium-high heat for 20 minutes.

SOY-GINGER DIPPING SAUCE Whisk all ingredients together in a small bowl, or whisk together liquids only and serve ginger on the side.

ASSEMBLY Place dumplings on a large serving platter. Sprinkle sesame seeds over top and serve with sauce.

PEARL DUMPLINGS

1 cup glutinous (sweet) rice, soaked overnight in cold water
1 lb ground pork
6 water chestnuts, coarsely chopped
2 cloves garlic, minced
1 egg
2 tsp finely grated ginger
1 tsp cornstarch
¼ tsp ground white pepper
1 tsp kosher salt, plus extra to taste
2 tsp soy sauce
2 tsp Shaoxing rice wine
1 tsp sesame oil

SOY-GINGER DIPPING SAUCE

1 Tbsp finely grated ginger
2 Tbsp soy sauce
2 Tbsp dark rice vinegar
¼ tsp sesame oil

ASSEMBLY

Pearl Dumplings (see here)
Toasted white and black sesame seeds, for sprinkling
Soy-Ginger Dipping Sauce (see here)

Moroccan Bites Tagine

Latifa Ghafai (c), Wafa El Maroudi (R), and Nadia El Maroudi (L)

IT'S A family affair at this compact café, filled with the aromas and artwork of an ancient country. Morocco's deep culinary roots are front and center as sisters Nadia and Wafa El Maroudi aid "Mama" Latifa Ghafai with kitchen duties to deliver authentic dishes, course after course. The sisters also take care of the front of the house, offering guests mint tea poured ahigh from ornate silver pots into tiny cups—a warm welcome and sign of good things to come.

A 2011 feature on Guy Fieri's *Diners, Drive-Ins and Dives* changed the trajectory of the restaurant—each time the segment airs on Food Network, the tables fill. Lamb dominates the menu—roasted, stewed, ground into kefta, and grilled as kebabs—as do other time-honored dishes such as delicate handmade couscous, aromatically spiced eggplant, and slow-cooked tagines such as lamb shanks with prunes (see page 162). Imported earthenware tagines line shelves and countertops, available for sale and encouraging guests to cook the cuisine at home. And a display case of Nadia's elegant cakes and honey-soaked and nut-filled pastries reminds guests to save room for dessert. During Ramadan, Moroccan Bites Tagine bustles after sundown, proving that those who know the cuisine are as impressed with the food as those who have newly "discovered" it.

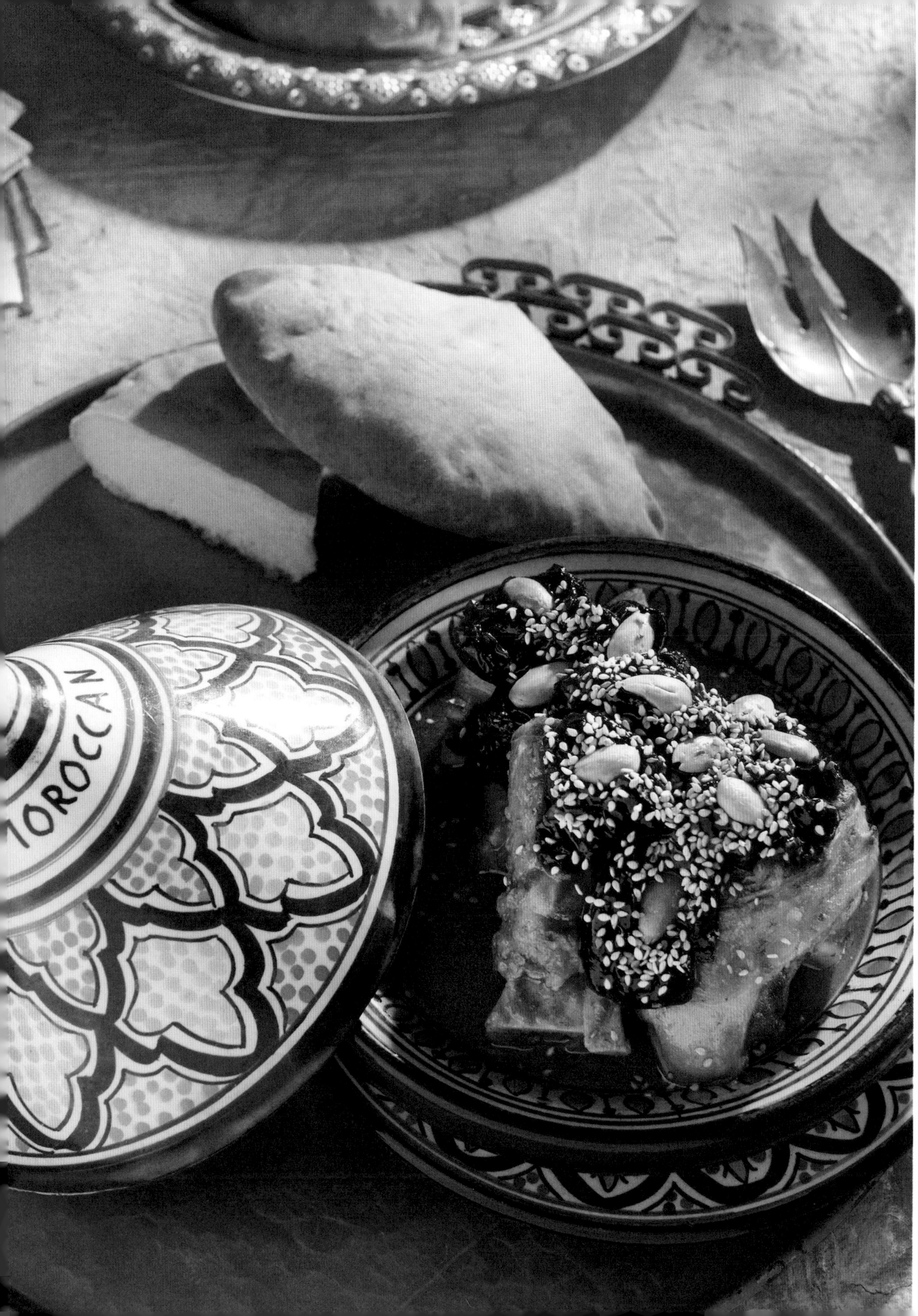

MOROCCAN BITES TAGINE Lamb Shanks with Prunes, p. 162

Lamb Shanks with Prunes SERVES 4

LAMB SHANKS

¼ cup olive oil

4 lamb shanks, 6–8 inches long each

1 large onion, chopped

1 Tbsp ground ginger

Kosher salt and black pepper, to taste

2 (4-inch) cinnamon sticks

Pinch of ground cinnamon

1 Tbsp chopped Italian parsley

1 Tbsp honey

PRUNES

12 dried prunes

6 (4-inch) cinnamon sticks

2 Tbsp sugar

Pinch of ground cinnamon

Pinch of ground nutmeg

1 Tbsp olive oil

2 tsp orange blossom water or
  rosewater

ASSEMBLY

Lamb Shanks (see here)

Prunes (see here)

Toasted almond slivers, for sprinkling

Toasted sesame seeds, for sprinkling

LAMB SHANKS Heat oil in a large Dutch oven over medium-high heat. Add lamb and onions and sauté for 5–10 minutes, turning lamb to cook on all sides. Season with ginger, salt, and pepper.

Pour in enough water to just cover lamb. Add cinnamon sticks, ground cinnamon, and parsley and bring to a boil. Reduce to medium-low heat, cover, and simmer for 30 minutes, until lamb is fork tender.

Remove lid and cook for another 5–10 minutes, until liquid has reduced to the desired gravy consistency. Stir in honey and cook for 2–3 minutes to meld flavors.

PRUNES In a medium saucepan, combine all ingredients and add enough water to cover prunes. Bring to a boil over medium-high heat, stirring to dissolve sugar. Reduce to medium-low heat and simmer for 5 minutes, until the mixture is brown and shiny.

ASSEMBLY Place lamb shanks and their gravy in a large serving bowl. Spoon prunes and a bit of juice on top. Sprinkle with almonds and/or sesame seeds.

Meshoui SERVES 4–6

Make 10–12 slits all over the lamb. Place lamb in a large roasting pan.

In a small bowl, combine turmeric, salt, pepper, garlic, and saffron. Add enough water to make a paste. Rub paste onto lamb and into the slits. Top lamb with onions, then pour a cup of water into the pan.

Seal the pan tightly in a layer of food-grade, oven-safe plastic wrap and a layer of aluminum foil. Refrigerate overnight or at least 2 hours.

Preheat oven to 375°F. Do not use convection setting.

Transfer the pan from the refrigerator directly into the oven and roast for 2 hours, until fork tender. Test doneness by peeling back some of the wrap. If more cooking time is required, add another 1 cup water, reseal the pan tightly, and cook for another 30 minutes or until tender. Allow lamb to rest in the pan for at least 10 minutes before serving.

Plate lamb, vegetables, and rice on a large platter. Spoon lamb juice on top or pour it into a gravy boat for individuals to serve themselves.

1 (4–5-lb) lamb shoulder or leg
1 Tbsp ground turmeric
1 tsp kosher salt
1 tsp white pepper
1 tsp garlic powder
5–6 saffron threads
1 large onion, sliced
Roasted vegetables, to serve
Plain rice, to serve

NOLA
Brunch & Beignets

Pieter Kaars-Sypesteyn and Susan Kaars-Sypesteyn

CHEF PIETER KAARS-SYPESTEYN grew up watching his parents run two restaurants in New Orleans and had no interest in the food industry. His love of illustrating drew him to art school in California, where he met and fell in love with his soulmate (Susan) and began to question his career choice. Pieter and Susan eventually moved to San Antonio, near his mother's family roots, and he started to train in restaurant kitchens from the bottom up. Soon, the couple struck out on their own, selling New Orleans cuisine from their Where Y'at food truck. After lines formed for the crunchy po'boys, buttery BBQ shrimp, fried boudin balls, and puffy beignets, loyalists spurred the couple to open a restaurant. NOLA was born, leaving behind truck life but not the recipes.

The brilliant concept of New Orleans–style big brunch decadence is a unique proposition in a city overrun with breakfast tacos. Set in a brightly painted house on a side street off the nightlife area of the St. Mary's strip, NOLA exudes the relaxed,

porch-sitting charm of New Orleans. Fans enjoy fresh-fried beignets all day, sauced omelets, po'boys, and sweet, ooey-gooey pancakes.

There's more. Not only are the couple successful restaurateurs, they also happen to be good fellow citizens. Their Third Coast Charities advocates for community change through action, building relationships between residents and businesses and funding neighborhood events and projects. The couple live out their values, doing good for others whenever and however they can.

Bread Pudding French Toast with Berry Compote and Almond Raisin Granola SERVES 8

This bread pudding can be served on its own. You can use store-bought granola if time is short, but you'll miss out on this outstanding homemade recipe, which happens to be made with Steen's cane syrup. ("The most amazing syrup on Earth," according to chef Pieter.)

BREAD PUDDING
Nonstick cooking spray
4 cups whole milk
1¾ cups sugar (divided)
7 eggs
1 Tbsp vanilla extract
1 tsp kosher salt
½ tsp ground cinnamon
Zest and juice of 1 orange
1 (12–16-oz) loaf French bread,
    torn into half dollar–sized pieces

GRANOLA
1 cup sliced almonds
1 cup quick oats
½ cup golden raisins
2 Tbsp dark brown sugar
2 Tbsp Steen's cane syrup
    or molasses
2 Tbsp honey
2 Tbsp apple juice
2 Tbsp butter, melted
1 tsp vanilla extract
½ tsp kosher salt

BREAD PUDDING Preheat oven to 375°F. Spray a 9- x 12-inch glass or ceramic baking dish with nonstick cooking spray.

In a large saucepan, heat milk and half the sugar over medium heat. Stir until sugar is dissolved and the mixture begins to steam. Do not let it boil over. Set aside.

In a large bowl, beat eggs and remaining sugar. Add vanilla, salt, cinnamon, and orange zest and juice. Slowly whisk in the milk-sugar mixture, a ladle at a time, until well combined. Add bread, mixing it in until well combined.

Pour the soaked bread mixture into the baking dish, using a spatula to lightly flatten the surface. Bake on the center rack for 1 hour, until the top is evenly browned and bread pudding has risen evenly. If the top gets too dark, cover it loosely with aluminum foil. Set aside to cool at room temperature for 1 hour, then refrigerate overnight. (If using the same day, rest the bread pudding for at least 1 hour before cutting it or it will fall apart.)

Once thoroughly chilled, slice bread pudding into 8 equal slices. Set aside.

GRANOLA Preheat oven to 350°F.

In a large bowl, combine all ingredients. Transfer to a baking sheet and spread out into a single layer. Bake for 10 minutes, then stir. Bake for another 10 minutes, then stir again. Bake for a final 5–10 minutes, until granola is golden brown. Set aside to cool to room temperature. Makes about 3 cups.

BERRY COMPOTE In a medium saucepan, combine berries, sugar, lemon, and salt. Simmer over low-medium heat for 5 minutes, stirring frequently to prevent the bottom from sticking and burning.

Add butter, stir, and cook for 1 minute. Remove from heat and set aside to cool to room temperature. Leftover compote can be stored in an airtight container in the refrigerator for up to a week.

EGG BATTER Place all ingredients into a bowl and whisk well. Set aside.

BREAD PUDDING FRENCH TOAST Heat a large cast-iron or nonstick skillet over medium heat. Add 1 tablespoon butter to the skillet. While butter is melting, dip 2–3 slices of bread pudding into egg batter, coating all sides. Add battered bread pudding slices to skillet and cook for 3–4 minutes, until golden brown. Melt another ½ tablespoon butter in the pan and flip the bread pudding. Cook for another 3–4 minutes, until golden brown and warmed through. (If needed, lower heat to prevent bread pudding and butter from burning.) Repeat with remaining slices.

ASSEMBLY Place cooked bread pudding slices on individual plates or a large serving platter. Add a generous portion of berry compote and granola on top. And if you're serious about this brunch thing, finish the dish off with confectioners' sugar and whipped cream (or ice cream).

BERRY COMPOTE
1 lb mixed frozen berries
1 cup sugar
½ lemon
½ tsp kosher salt
½ cup (1 stick) butter

EGG BATTER
4 eggs
2 Tbsp sugar
1 tsp ground cinnamon
¼ cup whole milk

BREAD PUDDING FRENCH TOAST
Bread Pudding (see here)
Egg Batter (see here)
½ cup (1 stick) butter, as needed

ASSEMBLY
Bread Pudding French Toast
   (see here)
Berry Compote (see here)
Granola (see here)
Confectioners' sugar, to serve
Whipped cream or vanilla bean
   ice cream, to serve

Oyster and Egg Rockefeller Serves 6–8

This is a variation on the classic Oyster Rockefeller: a dish of oysters on the half shell, traditionally topped with a buttery green sauce and breadcrumbs, then baked. The chef recommends baking the potatoes a day in advance.

ROCKEFELLER SAUCE

2 Tbsp neutral oil such as avocado oil

6–8 slices bacon, diced (4 oz)

½ yellow onion, finely chopped (½ cup)

¼ cup finely chopped green bell pepper

2 Tbsp finely chopped celery

4–6 cloves garlic, minced

¼ cup white wine or water

¼ cup (½ stick) butter, cubed

¼ cup all-purpose flour

2 tsp kosher salt, plus extra to taste

1 cup whole milk

⅔ cup heavy cream

6 oz raw spinach

CRISPY POTATOES

6–8 small Yukon Gold or very small baking potatoes, rinsed and patted dry

Corn oil

Kosher salt and black pepper

ROCKEFELLER SAUCE Heat oil in a heavy-bottomed saucepan over medium heat. Add bacon and onions and sauté for 3–4 minutes, until onions are translucent. Add peppers, celery, and garlic. Cook for another 3–4 minutes, until tender.

Pour in wine (or water) to deglaze the pan, scraping the bottom to release the caramelized bits (fond). Add butter and stir until just melted. Add flour and salt and stir well to make a paste (roux).

Pour in milk and cream and bring to a boil, frequently scraping the bottom to prevent scorching. Add spinach and season with salt. Cook for 3–4 minutes, until spinach has wilted. Remove from heat.

Transfer the mixture to a blender and purée until smooth. Set aside until ready to use.

CRISPY POTATOES Preheat oven to 400°F.

Bake potatoes for 45 minutes until fully cooked. (Alternatively, if you're in a hurry, cover the potatoes with a damp paper towel and microwave them for 8–10 minutes, until cooked through.)

Heat oil in a cast-iron skillet over medium heat, then add potatoes. Using a durable spatula or the bottom of a small saucepan, smash them into the skillet until they are half their original size and the skin has torn. Do not completely pulverize them.

Season with salt and pepper, then cook for 3–4 minutes, until browned. Flip and cook for another 3–4 minutes, until golden brown with a crispy skin. If potatoes begin to stick to the pan, lift with a spatula, add a little more oil, and continue browning. Season with more salt and pepper, then set aside.

FRIED OYSTERS Heat oil in a deep fryer or deep saucepan over medium heat to a temperature of 375°F. If the oil is smoking, it's too hot.

Place oysters in a bowl. Sprinkle a few tablespoons flour at a time onto oysters to create a sticky coating. The oyster liquor should appear a little milky and slightly thicker. Don't create a batter.

Place Fish Fri in a separate medium bowl. Place a few oysters at a time into the Fish Fri and toss well. Set aside to rest in the breading for 1 minute to create a better coating. Shake off excess breading.

Working in small batches to avoid overcrowding and averting your face from the hot oil, carefully lower oysters into oil and deep-fry for 1 minute, until golden brown. Do not overcook them; otherwise, they will be tough. Using a slotted spoon, transfer oysters to a paper towel–lined plate and keep warm.

Used oil can be strained and reserved for sautéing. Don't worry; it won't taste like oysters.

ASSEMBLY Bring a large saucepan of water to a boil. Add vinegar and salt. One by one, break an egg into the water and poach for 3 minutes, until the whites are set and the yolks still runny. Lift out. Set aside and keep warm. (Alternatively, fry eggs sunny-side up, then set aside and keep warm.)

Place a small pile of spinach in the center of each plate. Top with one crispy potato. Place 5–6 fried oysters around the potato and sprinkle bacon around the plate. Top potato with an egg and Rockefeller Sauce. (If you're preparing the eggs sunny-side up, place sauce on potato and top with egg.) Garnish egg with a little smoked paprika and scallions (if using). *Bon mange!*

NOTE >> If you cannot find Zatarain's Crispy Fish Fri, or prefer to make your own, combine cornmeal, corn flour, your favorite Cajun seasoning blend, and salt. (The chef uses Bob's Red Mill cornmeal and corn flour.) You can also add a little rice flour to make it even crispier.

FRIED OYSTERS
Peanut or corn oil, for deep-frying
30–40 gulf oysters (about 1 qt), shucked
½ cup all-purpose flour
1½ cups Zatarain's Crispy Southern Fish Fri (see Note)

ASSEMBLY
1 tsp white vinegar
1 tsp kosher salt
12–16 eggs
14 oz baby spinach
Crispy Potatoes (see here)
Fried Oysters (see here)
12 slices bacon, cooked to be crispy and cut into 1-inch pieces
Rockefeller Sauce (see here), heated up
Smoked paprika, for garnish (optional)
Thinly sliced scallions, for garnish (optional)

Sea Island
Shrimp House

*Chrissy Anthony
and Barclay Anthony*

ONE OF the city's most treasured seafood spots, Sea Island thrives because of the quality of seafood, the efficiency of the scratch kitchen, and the value of the meals. Sea Island was founded by Chrissy and Dan Anthony in 1965, and son Barclay continues to provide the business with the loving care his parents built it on.

Fresh wild-caught shrimp arrive daily from the Gulf Coast, netted by dedicated shrimp boats run by multigenerational shrimpers. Shrimp are the menu's centerpiece—grilled in tacos; combined with crab, corn, and potatoes in a Cajun boil; stewed in gumbo; and so much more. Other fresh water and ocean fish and seafood are treated well, minimally manipulated, and generously portioned. You'll even find chicken and beef entrées on the menu, including a juicy Angus burger (that can be topped with grilled shrimp, of course). Fresh-daily veggies and sides, including garlicky steamed spinach and comforting jalapeño-cheddar cornbread, taste like home.

The food reels us in, and the friendly staff is what keeps San Antonio anchored to this charming mini-chain. The family remains very involved in the operations, too. On a busy Friday night, you might find Chrissy greeting patrons at the Rector Street location.

Ceviche SERVES 8

The beauty of homemade ceviche is that you can make it as spicy as you please.
Want more heat? Add more pickled jalapeños. Want to cool off a bit? Cut back on them.

Bring a gallon of water to a boil in a large saucepan.

Place fish in a shallow pan. Pour just enough boiling water over fish to cover. Cover pan with aluminum foil and set aside for 5 minutes, until fish is opaque. Drain.

Transfer fish to a large glass bowl.

In a separate bowl, combine lime juice and 2½ tsp salt. Pour over fish, then cover and refrigerate overnight.

Drain juices. Add jalapeños, tomatoes, onions, cilantro, remaining 1 teaspoon salt, black pepper, and oil. Mix gently. Carefully stir in avocados.

Serve with tortilla chips (or saltines).

1½ lbs mild white fish such as wild Alaskan pollock, mahi mahi, cod, or halibut, cut into 1-inch pieces

1½ cups lime juice

3½ tsp kosher salt (divided)

2 pickled jalapeño peppers, diced into ¼-inch pieces

2 large tomatoes, diced into ¼-inch pieces (2 cups)

1 red onion, diced into ¼-inch pieces (¾ cup)

3 Tbsp chopped cilantro

1 tsp black pepper

½ cup olive oil

2 avocados, cut into ½-inch cubes

Thick tortilla chips or saltines, to serve

Broiled Oysters with Bacon and Parmesan
SERVES 8 AS AN APPETIZER

Texas Gulf oysters are a seasonal delight. They're plumper and more buttery than their East or West Coast cousins. As outstanding as they are raw on the half shell, this preparation takes advantage of their size to pile on additional flavor.

Preheat broiler to 450°F.

Place shucked oysters on the half shell on a baking sheet. Combine bacon, saltines, Parmesan, and parsley in a small bowl. Top oysters with an even amount of the mixture and a slice of butter. Broil for 5 minutes, until golden brown.

Serve with lemon wedges and slices of French bread.

2 dozen fresh oysters, shucked on the half shell

1½ cups cooked and finely chopped bacon

2 sleeves saltines, crushed (about 80)

1½ cups shredded Parmesan

Bunch of Italian parsley, finely chopped

1 cup (2 sticks) butter, cut into 24 slices

2 lemons, cut into wedges, to serve

1 loaf French bread, sliced, toasted, and buttered, to serve

Sichuan House

Kristina Zhao (c), *Jian Li* (R), *and Hua Rong Fan* (L)

KRISTINA ZHAO set out to demystify Sichuan cooking when she and her father, Ye, opened Sichuan House in 2015. It worked, thanks to her detailed menu tagged with key terms to identify flavors as tangy, smoky, savory, sweet, spicy, aromatic, and fresh and light. As the curious became converts and spread the word, this little restaurant doubled in size.

The menu also offers whimsically on-target translations of dish names, such as "Sweet but Spicy Peanuts," "Pock-Marked Mother Chen," and "Hands-Folded Sichuan Wontons." These heirloom recipes express the complex flavors of a historic culinary region, which boasts twenty-four distinct flavor profiles and fifty-six cooking methods that have dominated tables for more than five thousand years. Yes, history is ingrained in every dish, but it's the creative modern touches that set Sichuan House apart—as evidenced in the décor, Kristina's wine-pairing meals (which also show off the versatility of the cuisine), and the skills of the kitchen headed by executive chefs Jian Li and Hua Rong Fan.

Kristina also opened Dashi on the opposite side of town, introducing new dishes and another detailed menu to a new audience. But it is her family's main business, a well-stocked Chinese grocery, which continues to aid the efforts in both kitchens and provide hard-to-find items so essential to the cuisine. And we're all the better for it.

Sautéed Green Beans SERVES 2–4

Generally, these beans are flash fried before they're finished in the wok to speed up the process. Designed for home cooks, this lighter version has the beans roasted first. The flavor and texture remain the same, and the bonus is a healthier meal.

1 lb green beans, ends trimmed
½ Tbsp + ½ tsp neutral oil such as soybean oil (divided)
1 tsp finely chopped ginger
2 tsp chopped scallions
2 tsp preserved mustard greens (preferably Sichuan Yibin), rinsed well
1 clove garlic, minced
Pinch of sugar, to taste
Pinch of salt, if needed
Shaoxing rice wine or dry sherry

Preheat oven to 475°F.

In a small bowl, toss beans in ½ tablespoon oil. Transfer to a baking sheet. Spread out in a single layer and roast for 5–10 minutes, until crisp-tender.

Place ginger, scallions, mustard greens, and garlic in a wok and quickly stir-fry on medium-high heat for 20 seconds. Add beans and the remaining ½ teaspoon oil and toss well. Season with sugar and salt and sauté for another 25 seconds. Remove from heat and stir-fry for 5 seconds. Add a splash of wine (or sherry) and toss again.

Transfer to a serving plate and serve immediately.

Garlic Noodles SERVES 2

This garlic noodles dish makes for a quick and satisfying vegetarian meal. Go beyond bean sprouts and use whatever fresh veggies you have in the fridge: spiralized carrots, zucchini ribbons, and even crunchy celery batons to offset the heat.

Cook noodles according to package directions. Drain well.

Place noodles in a medium bowl. Toss in vegetable oil to prevent them from sticking together.

In a small bowl, whisk Chinese chili oil, peppercorn oil, vinegar, and sesame oil. Whisk in chili flakes, sugar, ginger, garlic, and peppercorn powder. Season with salt and mix well. Pour the mixture over noodles and toss to coat. Add scallions, bean sprouts, and other vegetables. Toss, then serve.

NOTE >> Chinese chili oil is a delicious and aromatic condiment made with oil, toasted Sichuan chili flakes, and aromatic spices such as star anise, cinnamon, bay leaves, and peppercorns. The solids sink to the bottom of the jar, so it's easy to use just the oil from the top and spoon solids from the bottom as needed. It's not to be mistaken with Sichuan peppercorn oil, a slightly floral and almost lemony oil with mouth-tingling effect. Both are available in Asian grocery stores.

4 oz noodles such as ramen, lo mein, or any wheat flour noodle

½ tsp vegetable oil

3–4 Tbsp Chinese chili oil without flakes (see Note)

3 Tbsp Sichuan peppercorn oil (see Note)

2 Tbsp black Chinese vinegar (available in Asian grocery stores)

2 tsp sesame oil

2 Tbsp toasted chili flakes from chili oil (see Note)

2 Tbsp sugar

1½ Tbsp grated ginger

1½ Tbsp grated garlic

½ Tbsp Sichuan peppercorn powder, to taste (available in Asian grocery stores)

Kosher salt, to taste

3 scallions, chopped

1 oz bean sprouts

Thin ribbons of your favorite vegetables

Smoke Shack
Meat Market
Chris Conger

PITMASTER CHRIS CONGER opened his Smoke Shack BBQ restaurant in 2014, four years after being heralded for the barbecue from his food truck. Conger's fans requested access to the locally produced meats he cooked with, so he began sourcing more meat from area ranchers and opened Smoke Shack Meat Market next to his BBQ restaurant.

Reminiscent of old-school local butcher shops and corner stores, the market features a front-and-center display case filled with prime cuts of Wagyu and Angus beef, pastured local lamb, cage-free chicken, and pasture-raised pork. Thanks to the smokehouse shared with the restaurant, the array of house-cured and seasoned bacon offers a glimpse into the mind of a pro-smoker. Bacon seasoned with out-of-the-box flavors like honey-chipotle, maple espresso, chile pequín, and Cajun spice is sold by the pound. Specialty house-ground sausage links are just as creative—offerings can include Beef Enchilada, Kung Pao Chicken, Thai Green Curry, Maple Blueberry, and even Frito Pie. Shelves stocked with locally produced goods—dry rubs, sauces, pasta, black garlic, vinegars, and wines—make this a one-stop destination for cooks. And heat-n-eat meals fill a wall cooler for those occasions when cooking isn't on the agenda.

For Conger and his crew, the market is an extension of their commitment to supporting local producers, businesses, and friends—and to serving the best of everything to their happy fans.

Smoke Shack's
Famous Mac & Cheese SERVES 8

The brisket and sausage in this creamy pasta add a hint of smoke to the mix. You can also use any leftover smoked meats you have on hand for the same flavorful result.

Bring a large saucepan of salted water to a boil over high heat. Cook cavatappi according to package directions, until tender. Drain, then transfer to a bowl of ice water to cool. Drain again.

In the top pan of a large double boiler, combine Velveeta and milk and cook for 5 minutes, until cheese has melted. Stir frequently to avoid sticking or burning. Add cheddar and stir until melted. Add remaining ingredients and mix, until heated through. Stir in pasta and mix well to coat.

Serve immediately.

Salt
1½ lbs cavatappi pasta
1¼ lbs Velveeta cheese loaf
4 cups whole milk
1¼ cups shredded cheddar
1⅓ oz smoked brisket, chopped
1 oz cooked smoked sausage link, chopped
1½ tsp Cajun seasoning
1½ tsp black pepper

Smoked Chicken Salad SERVES 4

At family reunions, holidays, or for a simple home-cooked lunch, this savory-sweet chicken salad brings everyone to the table.

Preheat BBQ pit or smoker to 350°F.

Season chicken with salt and pepper. Cook chicken directly on the smoker rack for 30 minutes, until it reaches an internal temperature of 165°F. Set aside to cool. Cut into ¼-inch cubes.

Preheat oven to 350°F.

Spread almonds on a baking sheet and toast for 5 minutes, until golden brown. Watch the almonds carefully as they can burn easily. Set aside to cool.

In a bowl, combine mayonnaise and honey. Add chicken, almonds, celery, scallions, and cranberries and mix well. Cover and refrigerate until ready to serve.

2 lbs boneless, skinless chicken breasts
2 tsp kosher salt
2 tsp black pepper
⅓ cup sliced almonds
1½ cups mayonnaise
2 Tbsp honey
1 stalk celery, chopped
2 bunches scallions, green parts only, sliced diagonally (½ cup)
½ cup dried cranberries

South Alamode Panini & Gelato Co.

Josh Biffle

TEXAN JOSH BIFFLE took a circuitous route to become San Antonio's go-to gelatiere. While studying architecture at The University of Texas at San Antonio, he took a series of field trips to Tuscany that turned into a four-year, on-and-off love affair with gelato. He ditched architecture studies in Texas for culinary school in Italy, focusing on artisan gelato and apprenticing with a master gelatiere. When he returned to San Antonio, he spent a year selling his confections to great acclaim at a farmer's market while gathering a loyal fan base who couldn't get enough of the classic Italian flavors (such as *fior di latte*, *stracciatella*, and pistachio). Eventually, he opened a brick-and-mortar location in the artistic Blue Star complex.

Biffle remains true to his adopted Italian roots by importing as many regional ingredients as possible: Italian candied citrus peel and truffle sauce, pistachios from Sicily, hazelnuts from Piedmont, and walnuts from Sorrento. South Alamode has also become a magnetic lunch spot, where a warm panini is always followed by a cup or cone (plus a hand-pulled espresso for the road). If you can't get to the shop, you'll also find South Alamode gelato on the dessert menus at many of the city's top restaurants. Don't pass it up.

Watermelon and Elderflower Sorbet SERVES 10

Dextrose powder, stabilizers, and glucose syrup are natural ingredients that give Italian sorbet and gelato a smooth texture. They're available in health food stores and online.

All measurements are by weight or in metric because these recipes are from Italy. Most kitchen scales and measuring implements contain the measurements.

175 g cane sugar

10 g dextrose powder

3 g stabilizer such as carrageenan or guar gum

1 small seedless watermelon, peeled (500 g total)

45 g glucose syrup

60 mL elderflower liqueur (preferably St. Germain)

Semi-dry prosecco, to serve (optional)

Bring 225 mL water to a low simmer in a small saucepan over medium-low heat. The heat should be high enough to dissolve sugar, but not enough for water to come to a boil. (Every stovetop is different, so you may need to experiment with the heat level.)

Fill a large bowl with ice water.

In a medium bowl, whisk sugar, dextrose, and stabilizer. Stir the mixture into the water in the pan, whisking continuously, until powders have dissolved. Transfer the mixture to a separate bowl and chill syrup over the ice bath for 30 minutes.

Place watermelon, glucose, elderflower liqueur, and chilled syrup in a blender and blend until smooth.

Pour the mixture into a gelato or ice-cream maker and churn according to the manufacturer's directions, about 20–30 minutes. Transfer to a separate container and keep frozen.

Serve as is or drop small scoops of sorbet into champagne flutes and top with prosecco. *Buon Appetito!*

Toasted Cream Gelato with Peach-Amaretto Compote SERVES 15

Toasted cream adds ribbons of rich, caramelized flavor to this gelato.

TOASTED CREAM Pour cream into 2 (12-ounce) mason jars and screw on tops until finger-tight.

Insert a steamer rack into a pressure cooker and add 1 inch water. Place the jars in the pressure cooker, seal with the lid, and bring to full pressure over heat. Cook at full pressure for 2 hours, then remove from heat and allow to depressurize naturally. Carefully remove jars from the pressure cooker and set aside to cool. Refrigerate until chilled.

TOASTED CREAM GELATO In a stand mixer fitted with the whisk attachment, combine egg yolks, cane sugar, brown sugar, and salt. Whisk on medium-high speed for 3 minutes, until a uniform paste forms.

In a medium saucepan, combine 200 g toasted cream, milk, and glucose syrup and bring to a gentle boil over medium-low heat. Whisk in yolk paste and stir continuously until the mixture becomes an even consistency. Add gelatin and stabilizer and stir frequently. Cook until the mixture reaches 170°F.

Fill a large bowl with ice. Strain the mixture through a fine-mesh sieve into a separate bowl and place over the ice bath. Set aside until chilled.

In a third bowl, whisk remaining 300 g toasted cream until thick like whipped cream. Fold toasted cream into the cooled mixture.

Pour into a gelato or ice-cream maker and churn for 20-30 minutes. Transfer to a separate container and keep frozen. Refrigerate leftover toasted cream in a sealed jar for up to 3 days. Use it in coffee, with fresh berries, or wherever you would use heavy cream.

PEACH-AMARETTO COMPOTE Heat a large skillet over medium-low to medium heat. Place peaches, cut side down, in the skillet and evenly space apart. Sprinkle sugar over peaches and into the skillet and heat until sugar begins to melt and bubble.

Averting your face from the hot steam, carefully pour in amaretto. Cook for 3-5 minutes, until amaretto reduces by half. Using tongs, remove peach skins (which should come off easily) and discard. Add butter and toss until butter has melted and the mixture has become a rich glossy sauce. Remove from heat.

ASSEMBLY Scoop gelato into bowls and top with peach-amaretto compote.

TOASTED CREAM
1 qt heavy cream

TOASTED CREAM GELATO
140 g egg yolks (7-8 eggs)
140 g cane sugar
90 g light brown sugar
Pinch of salt
500 g chilled Toasted Cream (see here, divided)
550 g whole milk
50 g glucose syrup
22 g powdered gelatin
8 g stabilizer such as carrageenan or guar gum

PEACH-AMARETTO COMPOTE
10 peaches, skin on, pitted, and halved
125 g brown sugar
150 mL Disaronno Amaretto
30 g butter, cubed

ASSEMBLY
Toasted Cream Gelato (see here)
Peach-Amaretto Compote (see here)

South BBQ & Kitchen

Andrew Samia

ANDREW SAMIA built his reputation with burgers from his Crazy Carl's Burger Truck, established it with juicy pastrami and smoked bologna at Dignowity Meats, then firmly planted his flag as a skilled pitmaster at South BBQ & Kitchen in 2018. The Angus brisket and St. Louis–style pork ribs are prime examples of slow smoking, filled with deep flavor and pure meaty chew. The sides are also full of originality—for one, the dressed haricots verts with plump cherry tomatoes, crunchy almond slivers, and cotija cheese tops the charts. And the rustic Loaded Tater Tot Casserole? It's the baked potato's country cousin you secretly like a whole lot better. House-made pickled cucumbers, crunchy cabbage slaw, and tangy pickled red onion freckled with oregano cut through the fat.

The indoor communal tables offer a spectator's view of what others are eating as you dig into your tray, while the patio offers a sweeping vista of the rolling golf course fairways across the street. Ask the friendly counter folks if you can get a tour of the pit while you're there. You might get lucky enough to meet Samia and learn more about his craft.

South BBQ Borracho Beans SERVES 20

This quintessential accompaniment to South Texas barbecue is the most popular side at South BBQ & Kitchen. For the ultimate Texas barbecue taco, fill a hot tortilla with chopped brisket, ladle these beans on top, and finish with fresh salsa.

Spread out beans on a baking sheet and discard any foreign objects such as pebbles or broken beans. Rinse beans thoroughly in a colander.

Place beans in a large saucepan, then add tomatoes, ½ tablespoon salt, and enough stock to cover beans with liquid. Bring to a boil over high heat, then reduce to low heat. Cover and simmer.

Meanwhile, cook bacon in a skillet on medium heat for 3–5 minutes, until crispy. Using a slotted spoon, transfer bacon to the pan of beans.

To the skillet with the rendered bacon fat, add jalapeños, onions, oregano, cumin, and a pinch of salt. Sauté over medium heat for 3–4 minutes. Add garlic and sauté for another minute.

Add the jalapeño mixture, including bacon fat, to the pot of beans. Pour in beer and stir in half the cilantro. Simmer over low heat for 2–3 hours, until beans are tender, but not bursting. Season to taste with salt.

Transfer to a serving bowl and garnish with remaining cilantro. Serve.

4 cups dried pinto beans
5 Roma tomatoes, chopped
½ Tbsp kosher salt, plus more to taste
3 qts chicken stock
1 lb smoked bacon, cut into thick matchsticks, or lardons
3 jalapeño peppers, chopped
1 large yellow onion, chopped
1 tsp dried Mexican oregano
1 tsp ground cumin
5 cloves garlic, minced
1 (12-oz) lager beer (preferably Lone Star)
2 bunches cilantro, leaves and stems finely chopped (divided)

Chocolate Banana Cream Pie SERVES 8

This silky-smooth chocolate cream pie with banana whipped cream topping is the perfect complement to a Texas BBQ feast. Samia adds, "It is a fan favorite every year when we offer our annual Thanksgiving meal orders."

PIE CRUST Preheat oven to 350°F.

Pulse cookies in a food processor until coarsely ground. Continue to process for another 15 seconds, until finely crumbled. Add butter and pulse to combine.

Transfer the mixture to a 12-inch pie tin and press firmly into an even layer along the bottom and sides. Bake for 10 minutes. Set aside to cool completely.

FILLING In a medium saucepan, combine milk, cream, and salt. Bring to a simmer over medium-high heat, stirring occasionally to prevent the bottom from scorching.

In a bowl, whisk sugar, cornstarch, and egg yolks, until smooth and creamy. Quickly whisk in 1 cup of the hot cream mixture into the egg mixture (to temper the egg yolks). Slowly whisk tempered yolk mixture into the pan of cream. Reduce to medium heat and whisk continuously for 30 seconds, until the mixture thickens and large bubbles form on top. Remove the pan from the heat.

Whisk in butter and chocolate chips, until melted and smooth. Stir in vanilla. Pour the mixture into the pie crust. Cover with plastic wrap, pressing it onto filling's surface to prevent a skin from forming. Refrigerate for 4 hours, until filling is set and chilled.

PIE TOPPING In a chilled bowl of a stand mixer fitted with the whisk attachment, whip all ingredients except the chocolate for 1–3 minutes, until soft peaks form. (Alternatively, use a hand mixer.) Spread the mixture over top of pie.

Sprinkle with chocolate shavings and serve.

PIE CRUST

32 chocolate sandwich cookies (preferably Oreos)

⅓ cup (⅔ stick) butter, melted

FILLING

2⅔ cups whole milk

2 cups heavy cream

⅔ cup sugar

1 tsp kosher salt

⅓ cup cornstarch

12 egg yolks

½ cup (1 stick) + 3 Tbsp butter, cut into ½-inch chunks

13 oz semi-sweet chocolate chips

⅔ tsp vanilla extract

PIE TOPPING

2 cups chilled heavy cream

¼ cup confectioners' sugar

⅔ tsp vanilla extract

1 (3.4-oz) box instant banana pudding mix

Dark chocolate shavings, for garnish

Southerleigh Fine Food & Brewery

Jeff Balfour and Aaron Juvera

IT'S A brewery, oyster bar, Southern comfort food café, upscale chophouse, and Texas bayside restaurant. It's all of those things housed in the former nineteenth-century Pearl brewhouse.

Chef-owner Jeff Balfour had his hands full during the two-year renovation that began in 2013. The result is visually stunning, with enormously thick columns, steel girders, and brick walls, all to the view of his brewing vats on the second floor.

Balfour is a Galveston native and career fine-dining chef who has divined an impressive menu by combining seasonal and regional ingredients with Southern influences. The lightly seasoned and fried snapper throats, a popular starter and entrée, are a remarkable display of sweet, tender collar meat cooked to perfection. Balfour's legendary fried chicken, jalapeño-cheddar grits, and country-style whipped potatoes are tastes of the Deep South.

It's also pinkies up for the char-grilled rib eye finished with dark rum glaze. And let's not forget the Galveston Bay shrimp boil and that East Texas crawfish roll. Balfour and executive chef Aaron Juvera are undoubtedly on point when they call it *Texas cross-cultural cuisine*.

The friendly service, the flights of beer, and the outdoor dining point to the fair winds of a great dining experience that's making its own history.

Bacon Jam Deviled Eggs MAKES 40 HALVES

This popular dish is often ordered as a satisfying starter or snack with Southerleigh's array of house-brewed beer and local taps.

HARD-BOILED EGGS Fill a large saucepan with very cold water. Add salt and baking soda, stirring to dissolve. Bring to a boil.

Gently lower in whole eggs, one at a time. Reduce to medium heat and boil for 16 minutes.

Meanwhile, fill a large bowl with ice water. (See Note.) Transfer eggs to the ice bath and set aside for 10 minutes, until cool to the touch.

Peel eggs and halve lengthwise. Scoop out the yolks into a large bowl.

NOTE >> If you plan to peel the eggs immediately, give them a crack before cooling them in the ice water bath. This will aid the peeling process.

DEVILED EGG FILLING Add mustard, mayo, and capers to a food processor and blend until capers are roughly chopped. Add egg yolks and blend until smooth yet not whipped enough to hold a peak.

BACON JAM In a heavy-bottomed saucepan or Dutch oven, cook bacon and onions over medium heat, stirring occasionally, until fat is rendered and bacon is crispy and dark. Pour in maple syrup, vinegar, and hot sauce and mix well. Add sugar and stir to fully incorporate. Reduce to low heat and simmer for 3–5 minutes, until the mixture thickens. (See Note.)

NOTE >> More bacon fat will render during this process and float to the top of the mixture. It can be skimmed from the surface once the jam has cooled.

Stir in paprika and thyme. Remove from heat and set aside to steep for 5–10 minutes.

Remove thyme and cool bacon jam to room temperature. Transfer to an airtight container. Refrigerate unused bacon jam for up to 2 weeks.

ASSEMBLY Spoon filling into a piping bag with a #4 star tip. Pipe a tablespoon of filling into each egg white half. Top with a teaspoon of bacon jam. Garnish with parsley and smoked paprika.

HARD-BOILED EGGS
2 tsp kosher salt
1 tsp baking soda
20 extra-large or jumbo eggs

DEVILED EGG FILLING
2 Tbsp Creole mustard
1½ cups Duke's Mayonnaise
¼ cup capers, drained and rinsed
Hard-Boiled Eggs, yolks only (see here)

BACON JAM
1 lb bacon, finely chopped
1 lb onions, finely diced
½ cup pure maple syrup
¼ cup apple cider vinegar
¼ cup Crystal Hot Sauce
½ cup brown sugar
½ tsp smoked paprika
Sprig of thyme

ASSEMBLY
Deviled Egg Filling (see here)
Hard-Boiled Eggs (see here)
Bacon Jam (see here)
Chopped Italian parsley, for garnish
Smoked paprika, for garnish

Watermelon Salad with Whipped Goat Cheese and Tajin Pepitas SERVES 4

MINT VINAIGRETTE In a food processor, combine sugar, lemon juice, honey, and mustard. With the processor on, slowly stream oil into the bowl and mix until thick and emulsified with a low viscosity. Add herbs and pulse a few times to incorporate without breaking them down. Leftover vinaigrette can be stored in an airtight container in the refrigerator for a week.

TAJIN PEPITAS Preheat convection oven to 375°F. Line a baking sheet with parchment paper.

In a stainless-steel bowl, combine pepitas, Tajin, and 2 tablespoons water and toss evenly to coat. Evenly spread out pepitas on the baking sheet. Bake for 15 minutes, until water has evaporated and seeds are lightly toasted. Set aside to cool completely. Store in an airtight container and snack on any leftovers.

WHIPPED GOAT CHEESE Combine all ingredients in a stand mixer fitted with the paddle attachment. Whip on low speed for 2 minutes. Gradually increase to high speed and mix until smooth and thick.

ARUGULA SALAD Mix all ingredients in a bowl and reserve.

WATERMELON WEDGES Using a serrated knife, cut along the side of melon and remove rind and pith, section by section. Cut melon flesh into quarters, then cut each quarter into ¾-inch-thick slices. Reserve in a container until needed.

ASSEMBLY Swipe ½ cup whipped goat cheese along half of the inside rim of each of 4 shallow serving bowls. Arrange 3–4 slices of watermelon along the opposite side. Place arugula salad between goat cheese and watermelon. Spoon 2 tablespoons vinaigrette over watermelon. Sprinkle pepitas and salt over salad and watermelon. Artfully place cantaloupe balls (if using).

Serve immediately.

MINT VINAIGRETTE
¼ cup sugar
¼ cup lemon juice
1½ Tbsp honey
1 tsp Dijon mustard
1½ cups vegetable oil
½ Tbsp thinly sliced mint
½ Tbsp thinly sliced basil
½ Tbsp finely chopped curly parsley
1 tsp thyme leaves

TAJIN PEPITAS
1 cup pepitas
2 Tbsp Tajin (see page 19)

WHIPPED GOAT CHEESE
2 cups chèvre (soft goat cheese)
2 cups heavy cream
1 Tbsp finely chopped thyme
1 Tbsp finely chopped Italian parsley
1 Tbsp kosher salt
1 tsp lemon zest

ARUGULA SALAD
8 cups arugula
1 bunch curly parsley, most of the stems removed and left in florets
1 red onion, thinly sliced
2 large red radishes, thinly sliced

WATERMELON WEDGES
1 personal-size watermelon, halved

ASSEMBLY
Whipped Goat Cheese (see here)
Watermelon Wedges (see here)
Arugula Salad (see here)
Mint Vinaigrette (see here)
Tajin Pepitas (see here)
Flaked sea salt
Cantaloupe balls (optional)

Supper at Hotel Emma

John Brand

WHEN JOHN BRAND was named executive chef at Supper in the posh Hotel Emma, he was given carte blanche to marry his Midwestern farm ethos and love of spices with the abundance of Texas ingredients. Seasonal vegetables are always at the center of the table, with okra, olives, and fennel playing in a spicy tomato sauce in summer and harissa-roasted root vegetables heating things up in winter. Each season may introduce new ideas, yet the constant is the uncompromised flavor that lifts each element to its best, punctuated by house-made condiments, spice blends, and other culinary concoctions.

The lofty monochromatic dining room is contemporary and luxurious, accented with brass fixtures, wood tables, and tobacco-colored leather banquettes. A wall of floor-to-ceiling windows overlooks the dining patio and river. Daytime is bright and cheerful, evening a twinkle of joy.

Because it's a hotel restaurant, breakfast and lunch are also on at Supper. The menu offers plenty of options for sustaining a day of sightseeing with hearty omelets, pancakes, and pastries. At lunch, it's a top choice for extended business meetings where the food inspires creativity, and on-point service is never called into question.

Sunchoke Tostones with Fresh Herb Salad SERVES 4

Sunchokes, also known as *Jerusalem artichokes*, have a relatively low glycemic index, which makes them a great potato substitute for those watching their carb intake.

SUNCHOKE TOSTONES Place sunchokes in a saucepan of water. Bring to a boil, then reduce to medium-low heat and simmer for 30 minutes, until soft and pliable. Drain.

Preheat oven to 250°F.

Transfer sunchokes to a cutting board. Gently press them with a pan or spatula until they are just less than an inch thick and break slightly.

Heat oil in a cast-iron skillet over medium heat. Add sunchokes and sear for 3–5 minutes per side, until crispy and golden. If searing in batches, add more oil to avoid sticking. Transfer sunchokes to an oven-proof plate, then season with salt and pepper. Keep warm in the oven until needed.

FRESH HERB SALAD Place all ingredients except salt and pepper in a medium bowl and gently toss. Season with salt and pepper.

ASSEMBLY Arrange 3 warm tostones on each of 4 plates. Top with salad. Serve.

SUNCHOKE TOSTONES

12 sunchokes, scrubbed of visible dirt
2 Tbsp sunflower oil
Kosher salt and black pepper

FRESH HERB SALAD

2 avocados, thinly sliced
2 stalks celery, thinly sliced diagonally
1 green bell pepper, seeded, deveined, and cut into matchsticks
½ English cucumber, cut into half moons
9 sprigs Italian parsley, leaves only and torn
7 basil leaves, torn
5 sprigs mint, leaves only and torn
2 sprigs dill, fronds only
3 oz queso fresco
1 cup arugula leaves
½ cup Castelvetrano olives, pitted and quartered
½ cup extra-virgin olive oil
Juice of 2 limes
Kosher salt and black pepper, to taste

ASSEMBLY
Sunchoke Tostones (see here)
Fresh Herb Salad (see here)

Hoja Santa with Sweet Potato, Black Beans, Avocado, and Chile-Pepita Crunch SERVES 6

This healthy snack was inspired by the prolific springtime bounty of hoja santa leaves and vegetables found in small Oaxacan villages. Hoja santa is also known as *Mexican pepperleaf*, *root beer plant*, and *yerba santa*. Both fresh and dried leaves are generally available in Latin grocery stores, depending on the season. The fragrant, velvety leaves impart notes of anise, nutmeg, and black pepper to foods. If you can find only dried leaves, soak them in warm water to rejuvenate the flavor before use. If you have extra leaves, use them as a wrap to steam eggs, cheese, or vegetables—or in place of tortillas for tacos.

SWEET POTATO Preheat oven to 425°F.

Place sweet potato on a baking sheet lined with parchment paper and bake for 40-50 minutes, until easily pierced with a fork. Set aside to cool.

Remove skin, place potato in a bowl, and mash until smooth. Season with salt and pepper.

CHILE-PEPITA CRUNCH Combine all ingredients in a small bowl and mix well.

ASSEMBLY Using scissors, cut leaves into six 8-inch disks. Wash and dry.

Lay leaves on a cutting board, rough side up. Evenly distribute sweet potato into the center of each leaf, then top with a squeeze of lime. Add black beans, avocados, scallions, and 1 tablespoon chile-pepita crunch. Gently fold each leaf into a taco shape or roll into a dolma, tucking in the sides.

Garnish generously with remaining chile-pepita crunch and serve.

SWEET POTATO
1 sweet potato
Kosher salt and black pepper

CHILE-PEPITA CRUNCH
7 large cloves garlic,
    peeled and crushed
2 cups pepitas, shelled and toasted
¼ cup toasted sesame seeds
¼ cup toasted hemp hearts
1 tsp ground Morita chile powder
½ cup sunflower or avocado oil
Sea salt, to taste

ASSEMBLY
6 hoja santa leaves
1 mashed Sweet Potato (see here)
1 lime, halved
2 cups cooked black beans, warm
2 avocados, thinly sliced
3 scallions, thinly sliced
6 Tbsp Chile-Pepita Crunch
    (see here), plus extra for garnish

Sushihana

FROM LEFT TO RIGHT:
Jorge Estrada, Luis Amaya, Howard Hu, Eduardo Castellanos, Mario Ramos, and Daniel Beltran

SUSHIHANA IS a sushi lover's raw bar, a seafood lover's dock, a meat lover's corral, and an Instagram foodie destination. It's all of these things because operating partner Howard Hu, executive chef Mario Ramos, and their team members are perfectionists who import top-quality fish from Japan and Tahiti and source only the best ingredients for everything else from miso to beef.

Gourmets go gaga over the swoon-worthy traditional sushi, creative fusions of Asian flavors, and belt-loosening entrées. The sushi is more than you'd expect at a top-notch contemporary Japanese spot—both in the generous portions and artful presentation. And dishes such as grilled Duroc pork chop with apple-ginger chutney and grilled New Zealand lamb chops with wok-fried eggplant appeal to the carnivores.

It's not unusual to see buzzy dining tables loaded with nigiri, soba, steaks, chops, colorful rolls, tempura, and a few bottles of reserve wines. At those tables? The city's top restaurateurs, chefs, and purveyors, who, after all, know a good thing when they find it.

The Japanese have a word, *kaizen*, a philosophy which translates to "change for the better." Rooted in the belief that continuous, incremental improvement equates to substantial change over time, *kaizen* involves all employees in the business processes. Ramos attributes the restaurant's success and popularity to Howard and Susan Hu and their practice of *kaizen*. "They've created a culture of inclusion, and through that process, we've all been able to work together to set a course for Sushihana's unique sense of hospitality."

SUSHIHANA Yuzu Crudo, p. 205 and Grilled Medley Roll, p. 206

Yuzu Crudo SERVES 4

This Sushihana special is offered only a few times a year, and now, you can prepare it at home any time. Ask your local fish shop for sushi-grade fish and cooked octopus tentacle. High-quality yuzu juice can be found in Asian grocery stores.

YUZU MARINADE Place all ingredients in a blender and blend for 3 minutes. Season with more sugar if needed. (The salt and citrus flavors should dominate.) Strain the marinade and chill the liquid for at least 1 hour.

SUSHI-GRADE SEAFOOD Cube tuna into 8 pieces. Slice each scallop in half. Slice shrimp in half lengthwise. Slice snapper, salmon, and octopus into 8 equal pieces.

Arrange seafood on a baking sheet, cover with plastic, and refrigerate until ready to assemble.

VEGETABLES Arrange vegetables on a baking sheet. Cover and refrigerate.

YUZU CRUDO Transfer tuna to a separate dish and keep refrigerated.

Arrange 4 (16-ounce) food-grade deli cups, or equivalent containers with tight-fitting lids, on the counter. These will be the curing vessels. In each cup, place a piece of scallop and 2 pieces of shrimp. Top with red snapper, salmon, and octopus. Add 4 tomato halves and a piece of jalapeño and onion. Divide cucumbers evenly.

Pour chilled yuzu marinade equally among the containers. Seal and refrigerate for 2 hours to cure, shaking containers every 30 minutes. Do not leave longer, because that will fully cure the fish.

ASSEMBLY Drain marinade from each container into a bowl and reserve. Artfully plate seafood and vegetables. Add avocado and top with tuna. Spoon some reserved marinade over ingredients. Garnish with micro cilantro.

Serve immediately.

YUZU MARINADE
1 cup yuzu juice
½ cup fresh orange juice
½ cup fresh lemon juice
½ cup fresh lime juice
2 Tbsp ginger, peeled (about the size of a thumb)
2 Tbsp kosher salt
2 Tbsp sugar, to taste
¼ Tbsp white pepper
2 cloves garlic, peeled

SUSHI-GRADE SEAFOOD
4 oz bluefin tuna
2 (u-10) scallops
4 jumbo shrimp, peeled and deveined
4 oz Japanese red snapper
4 oz Scottish salmon
4 oz octopus tentacle, cooked

VEGETABLES
8 cherry tomatoes, halved
½ jalapeño pepper, quartered
¼ small cucumber, unpeeled and sliced into thin rounds
¼ small red onion, quartered

YUZU CRUDO
Sushi-Grade Seafood (see here)
Vegetables (see here)
Yuzu Marinade (see here)

ASSEMBLY
Yuzu Crudo (see here)
Avocado, thinly sliced
Micro cilantro, for garnish

Grilled Medley Roll MAKES 4 ROLLS

Sushi at home? Absolutely. It may take a few tries to perfect the technique, but even the "failures" will taste delicious. Making sushi is a fun activity when you gather around the table with friends and family. And because this beautiful roll is vegetarian, the ingredients won't break the bank. Note: You'll need a sushi mat to create this dish. They are easily found at most Asian supermarkets.

SUSHI-ZU

2 cups clear rice vinegar

7 Tbsp sugar

3 Tbsp kosher salt

½ orange, unpeeled and sliced into 3

SUSHI RICE

2 cups short grain rice (sushi rice)

¾ cup Sushi-zu (see here)

SPICY EEL SAUCE

1 cup Kikkoman Eel Sauce

3 Tbsp Sriracha

2 Tbsp olive oil

1 Tbsp Sushi-zu (see here)

VEGETABLES

3 large red bell peppers

Olive oil

Kosher salt

Black pepper

4 asparagus spears,
    each trimmed to 7 inches

8 scallions, each trimmed to 7 inches

1 large carrot

NOTE >> While you can purchase sushi-zu in an Asian grocery store, it will alter the taste of this recipe. Most sushi restaurants make their own sushi-zu to differentiate themselves from their competition.

SUSHI-ZU In a 2-quart plastic or glass container, combine vinegar, sugar, and salt and mix until sugar and salt have completely dissolved. Add orange slices, cover, and set aside at room temperature for at least 2 hours prior to use. Store in a sealed container at room temperature for up to a month.

SUSHI RICE Rinse rice 3–4 times until the water runs clear. Drain well.

Place rice and 2 cups water in a medium saucepan, cover, and bring to a boil over medium-high heat. Reduce to low heat and simmer for 10–15 minutes, until water is fully absorbed. Remove from heat, keep covered, and set aside to rest for 10 minutes. (Note: If using a rice cooker, simply combine rice and water and cook according to manufacturer's instructions.)

Transfer rice to a medium wooden bowl. (Wood conducts heat and moisture in a unique way and its use is a specific part of Japanese cooking.)

Spread rice into a layer and drizzle with sushi-zu. Using a wooden spatula, mix rice and sushi-zu with a gentle cutting motion. Turn rice every 10 minutes until steam is no longer visible and rice is room temperature. The key is to keep the rice moist by covering it with a damp towel between turns.

Cover the bowl and set aside at room temperature until needed. For ideas about using the leftover rice, see tip box.

SPICY EEL SAUCE In a small bowl, combine all ingredients and mix well. Refrigerate.

VEGETABLES Preheat a grill over high heat.

Rub bell peppers with oil, salt, and black pepper. Add peppers to the grill and grill on each side for 3 minutes, until blistered all over. Transfer peppers to a bowl and cover with plastic wrap. Set aside until cool to the touch.

Peel charred skin off peppers. Cut off the top and bottom and devein. Cut lengthwise into 16 rectangular strips, about 1¼-inch wide. Set aside.

Season asparagus with oil, salt, and black pepper. Grill for 2–3 minutes on each side, until al dente. Do not overcook. Set aside with peppers.

Season scallions with oil, salt, and black pepper. Blister on all sides for 3–4 minutes total, until soft. Set aside with other vegetables to cool, then cover and refrigerate.

Cut carrots into julienne matchsticks (⅛ x ⅛ x 2½ inches), place in water, and refrigerate for 5–10 minutes.

ASSEMBLY Fill a small bowl with water. For each roll, lay nori on a cutting board, with the shaggy side facing up. Dip your fingers in water and thoroughly dampen both hands.

Spread a golf ball size of rice evenly over the entire surface of the shaggy side of nori. Flip nori over and place 3 carrot matchsticks, grilled asparagus, and grilled scallions on the first third of the nori closest to you. Using your fingers, carefully lift nori edge closest to you and begin to roll. Fold nori over vegetables, tucking in veggies snugly. Finish the roll procedure until cylindrical with a tight seam. Use a sushi mat to tighten and shape the roll.

With the seam side down, alternate peppers and avocados across the roll. Using the sushi mat, press down and adhere peppers and avocados to the rice. Take care not to crush the ingredients. Tighten the outside edges by holding the sushi mat over the roll and gently pressing each edge inward. Repeat with remaining rolls.

Cut rolls into 8 equal pieces. Arrange on a plate, cut side up, and drizzle with sauce. Garnish with scallions and sesame seeds.

ASSEMBLY

2 (8- x 7-inch) sheets nori seaweed, cut in half to 4 x 7 inches
4 cups Sushi Rice (see here)
Vegetables (see here)
1 avocado, thinly sliced
Spicy Eel Sauce (see here)
4 scallions, thinly sliced, for garnish
4 tsp toasted sesame seeds, for garnish

VEGETABLE NIGIRI You can create vegetable nigiri with the leftover rice. Form rice into oblong beds, each about 3 x 1 x 1 inch. Top them with spears of grilled vegetables.

Tiago's
Cabo Grille

Matt Charbonneau

TIAGO'S FOUNDER Matt Charbonneau set out to bring the zesty flavors of Cabo San Lucas to San Antonio. He's achieved this through an expansive menu of wood-fired seafood, meats, and vegetables served on sizzling platters, tableside guacamole service, and tropical fruit salsas and cocktails—all served in a bright and airy dining room or on the comfortably shaded patio.

As the restaurant's popularity has grown over the years, the menu now includes street foods found late at night throughout Mexico. Seek out mini corn tortillas piled with beef, chicken, or shrimp; grilled mahi mahi tacos topped with crisp cabbage, chipotle mayo, and mango salsa; and fire-roasted corn on the cob loaded with butter, mayo, shredded cheeses, and chili seasoning. Tex-Mex is represented, too, through puffy tacos and enchiladas.

Tiago's doesn't leave anyone out of the experience: full gluten-free and vegetarian menus ease dietary decisions, plus there are plenty of options for kids. The Rim location is a busy happy hour spot (and voted best in the city on various polls). It certainly helps that HH starts at 2 PM and runs until 6:30, a timespan nearly as relaxing as sipping margaritas in a Cabo beach cabana.

TIAGO'S CABO GRILLE Akaushi Beef Skewers and Shrimp Brochette, p. 210 and Pineapple-Jalapeño Ranch Water, p. 213

Akaushi Beef Skewers and Shrimp Brochette SERVES 6

Akaushi beef, from a breed of Japanese red cattle, is prized for its delicate texture and buttery taste, thanks to its rich fat marbling. It is an expensive choice you won't regret making once you've tried it; if you can't find Akaushi, use the highest quality, most well-marbled beef you can find.

AKAUSHI BEEF SKEWERS
2½ lbs Akaushi or other premium
   sirloin, cut into 18 (2-inch) cubes
2 cloves garlic, peeled and crushed
1 cup brown sugar
¼ cup kosher salt
1 Tbsp black pepper
1 Tbsp ground cumin
1 Tbsp chipotle peppers in
   adobo sauce
4 cups pineapple juice
1 cup orange juice
½ cup + 2 Tbsp soy sauce
¼ cup vegetable oil
2 Tbsp ancho paste
1 Tbsp Worcestershire sauce
1 Tbsp balsamic vinegar
1 large red bell pepper, seeded,
   deveined, and cut into 6 squares
1 small white onion, cut into 6 wedges

SHRIMP BROCHETTE
18 jumbo shrimp, peeled with tail
   intact and deveined
2 jalapeño peppers,
   each cut into 9 strips
6 oz Monterey Jack cheese, cut into
   18 strips, each about ¼ x 2 inches
9 thin slices bacon, halved crosswise
1 large green bell pepper, seeded,
   deveined, and cut into 12 squares
1 small white onion, cut into 6 wedges

AKAUSHI BEEF SKEWERS Place beef in a wide, shallow container.

In a large bowl, combine remaining ingredients except bell peppers and onions. Pour marinade over beef, ensuring it is slightly submerged in the marinade. Cover and refrigerate for 12 hours.

On skewers, alternate beef, bell peppers, and onions.

SHRIMP BROCHETTE Top each shrimp with a strip of jalapeño and cheese. Wrap in a bacon slice.

On skewers, alternate 3 shrimp with 2 pieces bell pepper and 1 piece onion.

ASSEMBLY Preheat a grill over medium-high heat.

Add beef and shrimp to the grill. Grill beef skewers for 5–8 minutes total on all sides, until beef is cooked to your preference. Grill shrimp for 3–5 minutes total on all sides, until shrimp are opaque and cooked through.

Meanwhile, heat oil in a skillet over medium-high heat. Add red bell peppers, green bell peppers, onions, and corn and sauté for 3–4 minutes, until onions are translucent and peppers are softened. Stir in rice. Season with salt and pepper.

Place the rice mixture and buttered vegetables side-by-side on each serving plate. Top with a skewer of beef and a shrimp brochette. Serve with a lemon wedge on the side.

ASSEMBLY
Akaushi Beef Skewers (see here)
Shrimp Brochette (see here)
1 Tbsp olive oil
½ red bell pepper, seeded, deveined, and chopped (½ cup)
½ green bell pepper, seeded, deveined, and chopped (½ cup)
1 small onion, chopped (½ cup)
½ cup corn kernels
2 cups cooked white rice
Kosher salt and black pepper
Buttered vegetables, to serve
2 lemons, cut into wedges, to serve

Cucumber Chamoy Margarita and Pineapple-Jalapeño Ranch Water SERVES 1

Mix up your tequila routine with these spicy single-serve cocktails, inspired by Cabo San Lucas, Mexico. Tajin and chamoy sauce are generally available in grocery store produce sections or the international aisles.

CUCUMBER CHAMOY MARGARITA Muddle diced cucumbers in a cocktail shaker and add ice. Add tequila, Grand Marnier, lime juice, agave nectar, and chamoy sauce. Shake well.

Rim a tall 10–12-ounce serving glass with Tajin. Pour the mixture into the glass and garnish with cucumber slices.

NOTE >> Chamoy sauce is made from dried sour fruit that is salted and pickled.

PINEAPPLE-JALAPEÑO RANCH WATER Rim a tall 10–12-ounce serving glass with Tajin. Fill with ice. Add tequila, squeeze in lime juice, and drop lime into the glass. Add jalapeño, chopped pineapple (if using), and pineapple juice. Top with Topo Chico (or other sparkling mineral water).

CUCUMBER CHAMOY MARGARITA

6 slices cucumber, half diced
    and half thinly sliced (divided)
1½ oz Cuervo Tradicional Tequila
½ oz Grand Marnier
1 oz lime juice
1 oz agave nectar
½ oz chamoy sauce (see Note)
Tajin, to rim glass

PINEAPPLE-JALAPEÑO RANCH WATER

Tajin, to rim glass
1½ oz Dulce Vida Pineapple
    Jalapeño Tequila
Lime wedge
3 slices jalapeño peppers
2 Tbsp finely chopped pineapple
    (optional)
1 oz pineapple juice
Topo Chico or other sparkling
    mineral water

Metric Conversion Chart

VOLUME

Imperial or U.S.	Metric
⅛ tsp	0.5 mL
¼ tsp	1 mL
½ tsp	2.5 mL
¾ tsp	4 mL
1 tsp	5 mL
½ Tbsp	8 mL
1 Tbsp	15 mL
1½ Tbsp	23 mL
2 Tbsp	30 mL
¼ cup	60 mL
⅓ cup	80 mL
½ cup	125 mL
⅔ cup	165 mL
¾ cup	185 mL
1 cup	250 mL
1¼ cups	310 mL
1⅓ cups	330 mL
1½ cups	375 mL
1⅔ cups	415 mL
1¾ cups	435 mL
2 cups	500 mL
2¼ cups	560 mL
2⅓ cups	580 mL
2½ cups	625 mL
2¾ cups	690 mL
3 cups	750 mL
4 cups (1 quart)	1 L
5 cups	1.25 L
6 cups	1.5 L
7 cups	1.75 L
8 cups (2 quarts)	2 L

WEIGHT

Imperial or U.S.	Metric
½ oz	15 g
1 oz	30 g
2 oz	60 g
3 oz	85 g
4 oz (¼ lb)	115 g
5 oz	140 g
6 oz	170 g
7 oz	200 g
8 oz (½ lb)	225 g
9 oz	255 g
10 oz	285 g
11 oz	310 g
12 oz (¾ lb)	340 g
13 oz	370 g
14 oz	400 g
15 oz	425 g
16 oz (1 lb)	450 g
1¼ lbs	570 g
1½ lbs	670 g
2 lbs	900 g
3 lbs	1.4 kg
4 lbs	1.8 kg
5 lbs	2.3 kg
6 lbs	2.7 kg

LIQUID MEASURES
(for alcohol)

Imperial or U.S.	Metric
½ fl oz	15 mL
1 fl oz	30 mL
2 fl oz	60 mL
3 fl oz	90 mL
4 fl oz	120 mL

CANS AND JARS

Imperial or U.S.	Metric
14 oz	398 mL
19 oz	540 mL
28 oz	796 mL

LINEAR

Imperial or U.S.	Metric
⅛ inch	3 mm
¼ inch	6 mm
½ inch	12 mm
¾ inch	2 cm
1 inch	2.5 cm
1¼ inches	3 cm
1½ inches	3.5 cm
1¾ inches	4.5 cm
2 inches	5 cm
2½ inches	6.5 cm
3 inches	7.5 cm
4 inches	10 cm
5 inches	12.5 cm
6 inches	15 cm
7 inches	18 cm
10 inches	25 cm
12 inches (1 foot)	30 cm
13 inches	33 cm
16 inches	41 cm
18 inches	46 cm
24 inches (2 feet)	60 cm
28 inches	70 cm
30 inches	75 cm
6 feet	1.8 m

TEMPERATURE

(for oven temperatures, see chart in next column)

Imperial or U.S.	Metric
90°F	32°C
120°F	49°C
125°F	52°C
130°F	54°C
140°F	60°C
150°F	66°C
155°F	68°C
160°F	71°C
165°F	74°C
170°F	77°C
175°F	80°C
180°F	82°C
190°F	88°C
200°F	93°C
240°F	116°C
250°F	121°C
300°F	149°C
325°F	163°C
350°F	177°C
360°F	182°C
375°F	191°C

OVEN TEMPERATURE

Imperial or U.S.	Metric
200°F	95°C
250°F	120°C
275°F	135°C
300°F	150°C
325°F	160°C
350°F	180°C
375°F	190°C
400°F	200°C
425°F	220°C
450°F	230°C
475°F	245°C

BAKING PANS

Imperial or U.S.	Metric
5- × 9-inch loaf pan	2 L loaf pan
9- × 13-inch cake pan	4 L cake pan
11- × 17-inch baking sheet	30×45 cm baking sheet

Acknowledgments

Thank you to all the chefs, restaurateurs, and bar owners who came into this project with enthusiasm and joy, especially after such hard times; to Anthony Hernandez, for helping rework some of the crazier recipe reformatting; to my neighbors and friends, who willingly dined on my recipe tests and took home the leftovers; to Ross Burtwell, who gave me a front-row seat to a chef's drive for excellence; to Matt Charbonneau, for his friendship and support of this book; to the Figure 1 Publishing team, who put their faith in me; and to all the writing teachers in my school years, and the kind yet firm editors throughout my professional writing career.

Index

About the Author

JULIA ROSENFELD'S fascination with recipes and ingredients led her to pepper her writing career with gastronomic gigs, including fourteen years as the restaurant reviewer for *San Antonio Magazine*, a few as the local *Zagat* editor, and a few as the writing instructor at The Culinary Institute of America in San Antonio. In 2014, she coauthored her first cookbook, *Texas Hill Country Cuisine: Flavors from the Cabernet Grill Texas Wine Country Restaurant*, with chef Ross Burtwell. Since 2015, she has introduced countless guests to the city's chefs, artisans, and producers through her culinary tour company, Food Chick Tours (www.foodchicktours.com).

Figure.1